Best of Track and Field
from *The Coaching Clinic*

Compiled by the Editors of
The Coaching Clinic

Parker Publishing Company, Inc.
West Nyack, New York

Library of Congress Cataloging in Publication Data
Main entry under title:

Best of track and field from the Coaching clinic.

   1. Track-athletics coaching. I. The Coaching
clinic.
GV1060.5.B45   796.4'2   75-20058
ISBN 0-13-074880-3

Introduction

A great many fine articles on coaching Track and Field have appeared in *The Coaching Clinic* over the years.

Now, in response to many inquiries and requests from coaches across the country, here is the cream of the crop: 42 outstanding articles covering every phase of Track and Field competition.

In these pages, some of the nation's most knowledgeable and successful high school and college coaches provide you with a one-stop ready reference on the whole Track and Field spectrum—from sprints to shot put, hurdles to high jump, and all points between.

No matter how long you've been coaching Track and Field, you'll turn again and again to this invaluable anthology for tips on performance techniques, conditioning, practice schedules—even on selecting your athletes.

In all, you'll find this an indispensable addition to your professional library.

The Board of Editors of *The Coaching Clinic*

Table of Contents

Introduction 9

Part I

THE SPRINTS

1. A Program for Developing Sprint Men 15
   by Dick De Schriver
2. The Sprints: Start to Finish 19
   by Don Leek
3. Training the High School Sprinter 23
   by Douglas Hyke
4. Running the Sprints 29
   by Frank Zubovich
5. Tips on Sprinting Techniques 32
   by Dr. Leroy T. Walker
6. Workout Techniques for Sprinters 36
   Lindy Remigino

Part II

MIDDLE DISTANCE

1. Middle Distance Running 44
   by Steve Bartold
2. Selecting and Training the 440 Man 45
   by Sherman B. Hall

Part II
(cont.)

3. **Training the Quarter Miler** **49**
    by Don Kornhaus

4. **Coaching the 880-Yard Run** **55**
    by Ed Styrna

Part III
THE RELAYS

1. **The Sprint Relays** **63**
    by Maxie Hays

2. **Success in the Relay Events** **67**
    by Ronald Johnson

3. **The Relay as a Springboard to Success** **71**
    by Mark Cotton

4. **Coaching the 880 Relay** **77**
    by Steve Hansen

5. **Coaching the Relay Exchanges** **83**
    by Bobby Wicker

6. **Baton-Handling Skills in the 440 Relay** **88**
    by Jerry Martin

Part IV
THE HURDLES

1. **Selecting and Developing the High School Hurdler** **97**
    by Nate Long

2. **Coaching the Beginning Hurdler** **101**
    by Woody Turner

3. **Developing a Hurdler** **106**
    by Dean Benson

4. **Sprinting Through the Hurdles** **111**
    by Dr. Martin Pushkin

Part IV
(cont.)

5. **Drills for Hurdling Success**.............................**117**
   by Jack Keller

Part V
DISTANCE RUNNING

1. **Motivating the Miler**...................................**123**
   by Roger V. Hoy
2. **Training the High School Distance Man**.....................**127**
   by Leon Johnson
3. **A New Look at Distance Running**............................**131**
   by James Demo
4. **Conditioning the Distance Runner**..........................**136**
   by Larry McClung

Part VI
SHOT, DISCUS, JAVELIN

1. **Achieving Shot Put Form**................................**143**
   by Aubrey Bonham
2. **A 12-Pound Shot in a Size 16**............................**146**
   by David Star
3. **Strength Training for the Shot and Discus**....................**148**
   by J. L. Mayhew and Bill Riner
4. **Discus-Throwing Technique**.............................**154**
   by Ralph D. Maughan
5. **Javelin-Throwing Technique**............................**159**
   by Douglas Raubenheimer
6. **Common Faults in Throwing the Javelin**......................**163**
   by Ronald J. Hayes
7. **Specialized Isometric Training for the Javelin Throw**.......**168**
   by Raymond Frey

Part VII

POLE VAULT, HIGH JUMP

1. Developing the High School Pole Vaulter........................175
   by Don Harshbarger
2. Coaching the Pole Vault 179
   by Henry Thomson
3. Coaching Champion High Jumpers.............................185
   by Howard Bagwell
4. The "Western Dive" in High Jumping 188
   by Frank Zubovich
5. Teaching the "Fosbury Flop" to High Jumpers..............192
   by Doug Hyke

Part VIII

BROAD JUMP, TRIPLE JUMP

1. Developing the High School Broad Jumper 199
   by Steve Hansen
2. Isometrics and Step Running for Broad Jumpers 204
   by Gene Cox
3. Doubling in the Broad and Triple Jumps.......................208
   by Dr. Leroy T. Walker
4. Coaching the Triple Jump..210
   by Dr. Martin Pushkin
5. The Triple Jump in High School Track.........................213
   by John Arcaro

Part I
The Sprints

1

A Program for
Developing Sprint Men

by Dick De Schriver

Head Track Coach
East Stroudsburg (Pennsylvania) State College

*Dick De Schriver is Dean of the Faculty of Health Sciences
and Physical Education and head cross country and track
coach at East Stroudsburg State College. He also coached
track on the high school level at Aquin Central Catholic
(Freeport, Illinois) High School and St. Catherine's
(Racine, Wisconsin) High School. He says sprinters are
made, not born. Here's how he develops his.*

I am not saying that a coach can take a boy with average sprinting
talent and make a great sprinter out of him. But he can do this: With a
good program he can make that boy into a possible dual meet winner
and conference point scorer. It has worked with me. But the program
has to be planned for the *entire* season, and adhered to right on the
nose.

My program is divided into three parts:

1. The *conditioning* period (6 to 8 weeks).
2. The *intensive work* period (4 to 6 weeks).
3. The *sharpening* period (4 weeks).

VARIABLES: The variables in the program depend on your luck with weather, the availability of gym facilities, and the need and progress of the individual boy.

Here's what I do in each of the periods.

THE CONDITIONING PERIOD

The purpose of the conditioning period is to develop total body fitness. This is necessary if the boy is to stand up under the vigorous work coming up and to avoid serious injury when sprint work is introduced.

We stress calisthenics and relaxed, over-distance running. Calisthenics are more or less what you might expect: stretching exercises to help warm-ups and muscle loosening; reaction exercises (squat jumps, squat thrusts, leg striding and running in place); and body-building exercises (push-ups, sit-ups, pull-ups, flutter kicks and leg lifts).

Weather is something of a problem, so our running is done in sweat clothes and often in the streets.

NO SPEED: We do not emphasize speed; in fact, the boys usually have to be warned about running too hard. Relaxation is stressed and workouts are at a striding pace.

If serious flaws are noted in a runner's form, we correct them right away. We consider a flaw any action that interferes with the sprinter's forward movement or with his relaxation.

The workouts are of a repeat nature. We may do any of these things:

1. Three to four miles of wind sprints, in modified fartlek fashion (short sprints, jogging, walking).
2. Repeat 300's to 1000's, starting with four to six repetitions and gradually building up to 8 to 10 as the season progresses.
3. "Ups and downs"—400-600-800-600-400 yard runs.

KEEP MOVING: Between all repeats, we require the boys to keep jogging to prevent excessive cooling off.

We follow a weight-training program, three days a week. Each weight lift is done in three sets of ten repetitions. We use standard lifts, such as the military press, bench press, rowing motion, curls, ½ knee bends, and toe raises. The sprinters also run in place with 3-pound ankle weights, and we stress rapid, high knee action and correct forward lean.

STRENGTH MEANS SPEED: The positive relationship between strength and speed is now generally accepted in athletics. Our sprinters must be strong.

As soon as we have use of the gym, we teach the correct mechanics of the start. At first we allow individual experimentation, so that the boys will have comfortable foot spacing. Once the mechanics become a habit, and we have the boys in good physical shape, we practice starts for one-half the length of the basketball court. High school boys have a relatively short span of attention, so we limit these starts to 6 per practice session.

USE THE GUN: All practice starts are at top speed, with the starting gun and stopwatch. This prevents carelessness.

The aim of the conditioning period: strength and endurance.

THE INTENSIVE WORK PERIOD

The character of the intensive work period is endurance training gradually shifting to speed. We continue the starting workouts all through this period. Weight training is reduced to two days a week, and a few weeks before the first meet, mass calisthenics are dropped in favor of individual warm-ups.

ENDURANCE: Most sprinters do not realize the value of endurance. However, the finishing kick in the 100 or sustained speed in the 220 is based on endurance along with relaxation and strength.

A typical week's work would be:

Monday and Wednesday: Run repeat 330's, all out, with a 10-minute rest interval. After the opening meet (mid-April) we replace the Wednesday 330's with repeat 180's with an 8-minute rest. The number of repeats depends on the boy's condition. We do not like boys to become exhausted so they cannot run relaxed.

Tuesday and Thursday: Repeat 30 and 50 yard dashes, emphasizing starting. We often use a finish tape so that we can teach correct finishing techniques. On these days we devote time to baton passing for the relay men; this work is usually done at 9/10 speed.

Friday: If there is no meet, we run 180's, or work on individual needs of the boys. Occasionally we will substitute repeat 220's at 4/5 speed, so that we can stress proper relaxation and curve running form.

> MINIMUM TIME TRIALS: We keep time trials at actual racing distances at a minimum. We do not think a sprinter should be over-exposed to competitive situations which result in excessive stimulation. Save stimulation for the meets—particularly conference and district meets—where it will do the most good. We time only enough to determine event participation and relay team personnel.

The aim of the intensive work period: increased fatigue tolerance.

THE SHARPENING PERIOD

Here we are totally committed to speed work. In general, the plan is to blend starts, under-distance running, and baton passing. The sprinters do not lift weights during this period.

With a full meet schedule, the athlete requires more rest, and the work is reduced. On Monday, one or two 150's may be run; most of the practice sessions are devoted to running short sprints of 30, 50, or 70 yards in which starts and relaxed sprinting form are stressed. We spend more time on baton passing, and each practice ends with several 220's at 4/5 speed.

> VARIETY: As the season draws to an end, we add variety to the workouts to avoid their becoming boring to the boys. We may sprint the curves and jog the straightaways; we may handicap the sprinters; we may run relays. On the latter, we are careful not to contribute to fatigue on days of competition.

This is my sprint program. It has worked for me, because it is designed to fit in with the weather in my part of the world, the facilities I have, and the size of my squad. You must assess your own situation and organize and build around it.

2

The Sprints ...
Start to Finish

by Don Leek

Supervisor of Health, Physical Education, Recreation and Athletics
Gary (Indiana) Public Schools

In his years as head track coach at Roosevelt (Gary, Indiana) High School, Don Leek compiled a most impressive record: 5 state championships; 9 sectional championships; 7 regional championships; 9 city championships. He is presently supervisor of health, physical education, recreation and athletics for the Gary Public School system.

There was a time when being "gifted" was enough to enable a sprinter to win his event in every track meet he entered. Today, this is the farthest thing from the truth. It takes a fairly small "gift," a sizable knowledge of form, and one tremendous chunk of determination to be a champion. The "gift" is something no coach has control over; a boy has it or he hasn't. Determination can be increased in a boy with proper guidance, but it too is largely part of what a boy "has to offer." This leaves us with form. Form can be taught. It is the most important contribution a coach can make to his sprinters. It is the only one of the important ingredients for success that is really "teachable." Here is how we go about teaching it at Roosevelt:

POINT BY POINT: This is fundamental to my coaching philosophy: I believe that the only way to teach a boy form is to correct his natural mistakes *one at a time*. Never give him so many things to think about that he forgets the most important ones. With beginners, it is best to work from start to finish in logical sequence. If a boy has done a lot of running then it is all right to work on his shortcomings first—point by point.

The Start: The first thing to give attention to is proper block placement. Emphasis must be placed on *maximum power* from the front leg followed by *maximum quickness* with *balance* from the rear leg. Block placement and setting will differ individually, depending on body type and reaction time. Once the setting is established, measure each foot placement to the starting line and record the information.

The arm action at the start should be vigorous and complementary to the leg action. The arm action we like to emphasize is similar to a short uppercut in boxing.

The head and eye focal point will greatly influence body lean. We like to have our runners have their heads "hung over" at the "Mark" and "Set" positions so that they can achieve greater relaxation and concentration. The eyes are focused at a point about three or four feet ahead toward the finish. After the sprinter learns all the points of start form, the coach should work with him on balance and poise—poise doesn't come overnight. Diagrams 1, 2 and 3 illustrate the points of a good start.

Our method for developing the necessary power and quickness from the blocks in our sprinters is a series of repeat 10 yard starts. In the beginning we have our boys make these starts at ½ to ¾ effort and *alone*. As the runner progresses, the starts can be made at full effort. Later, team competition is added, but *only* after self-confidence is established in the boy.

NIP THEM QUICK: Occasionally, after team competition is added to the sprinter's workouts, he reverts to some of his old bad habits. On-the-spot corrections and encouragement

Diagram 1   **Diagram 2**   **Diagram 3**

Diagram 4   **Diagram 5**

will overcome this; it is a must, however, that the corrections and encouragement be given immediately so that faults do not have time to become ingrained in the boy.

"Body of the Race" Form: During the body of the sprint, I look for a definite, but smooth, transition from the explosive, vigorous action off the blocks to a smooth, picturesque, relaxed, high knee-actioned stride. Diagram 4 shows this phase of the race. The coach should give some attention to getting his runners to relax their facial muscles while they run. This will relax their neck and shoulder muscles. The fingers and hands should not be tightly clenched. This could easily bring tension to the arms and shoulders. If a boy shows great difficulty in relaxing, let him work at speeds slower than full effort until he begins to get the feel of *full* relaxation *without* loss of speed.

The Finish: During the last 10 to 15 yards of the sprint, I like to stress the need for a driving finish. This means a slightly exaggerated body lean forward and a drive *through* the tape rather than a lunge or leap *at* it. Many races have been lost at the tape because the runner did not drive through the finish. The technique we use to establish this phase is simple. We tell the boy to "think" through the finish and run through the tape. He must always imagine that the tape is a few yards ahead even when he is breaking it! The body lean should begin with the chin extended forward as if the runner is reaching for something just ahead. The arms should not be extended forward. They should be as near to the normal running position as possible.

TOO MUCH LEAN: If a runner appears to be off-balance or stumbles as a result of this technique, it is probably due to too much body lean. How much is enough? As much lean as the boy can manage without falling on his face (Diagram 5).

3

Training the High School Sprinter

by Douglas Hyke

Head Track Coach
Havre (Montana) High School

Douglas Hyke has been head track coach for the past 13 years at Havre High School, where his squads have a 89% winning record in dual and triangular meets. During that time his teams have won 25 major Invitational meets, 4 State Championships and 4 Eastern Montana Divisional Championships. Coach Hyke was named Montana Class A Coach-of-the-Year 4 times.

With one head coach and three assistants for about 100 track-and-field athletes, I find it works best to divide the events among the coaches, with each coach taking responsibility for three or four events. Of course, it becomes necessary for the head coach to provide direction for his assistants.

NOTE: I find this is best accomplished by the use of instructional booklets, which I have written for each event, based on information gathered from track clinics, articles, books, and experience. By means of these booklets, I can convey my ideas through the assistant to the athlete. The booklets can also be used by an athlete for self-instruction on technique.

Following is an example of an ''instructional booklet'' used for training sprinters. The material presented can be adapted to fit your own particular situation.

SPRINTER'S WARM/UP

The following warm-up drills should be performed each day. We start by jogging for 440 yards—and then we do the following exercises to a four count with ten repetitions: (a) trunk twister; (b) side straddle hop; (c) fingertip push-ups; (d) calf stretching drill; (e) hamstring stretching drill; (f) cross feet, reach down, and touch toes; (g) groin stretching exercise; (h) hurdlers' drill; (i) sit-ups with knees flexed; (j) leg raisers, stomach stretching exercise; (k) bottoms-up drill; (l) high kicks; (m) kneeling sit-ups.

NOTE: Our 1 ¾-mile warm-up drill is illustrated in Diagram 1 and is self-explanatory.

GENERAL WORKOUT SCHEDULE

Chart I shows our general workout schedule for midseason and late season. On each day, the athlete must make certain that he is warmed up properly.

STARTING

1. Use the same warm-up for meets that you use in practice.
2. Never take starts until your legs are in condition—about two weeks if you were participating in a winter sport.
3. Never take starts on cold days.
4. Make certain you are warmed up before you take a start.

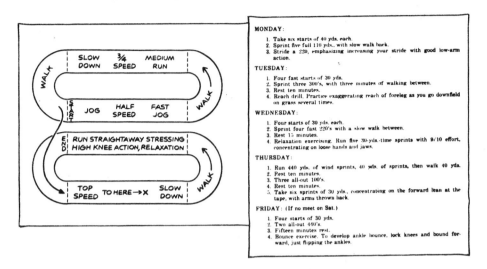

Diagram 1

MONDAY:

1. Take six starts of 40 yds. each.
2. Sprint five full 110 yds., with slow walk back.
3. Stride a 220, emphasizing increasing your stride with good low-arm action.

TUESDAY:

1. Four fast starts of 30 yds.
2. Sprint three 300's, with three minutes of walking between.
3. Rest ten minutes.
4. Reach drill. Practice exaggerating reach of foreleg as you go downfield on grass several times.

WEDNESDAY:

1. Four starts of 30 yds. each.
2. Sprint four fast 220's with a slow walk between.
3. Rest 15 minutes.
4. Relaxation exercising. Run five 30-yds.-time sprints with 9/10 effort, concentrating on loose hands and jaws.

THURSDAY:

1. Run 440 yds. of wind sprints, 40 yds. of sprints, then walk 40 yds.
2. Rest ten minutes.
3. Three all-out 100's.
4. Rest ten minutes.
5. Take six sprints of 30 yds., concentrating on the forward lean at the tape, with arms thrown back.

FRIDAY: (If no meet on Sat.)

1. Four starts of 30 yds.
2. Two all-out 440's.
3. Fifteen minutes rest.
4. Bounce exercise. To develop ankle bounce, lock knees and bound forward, just flipping the ankles.

Chart 1

THE ROCKET START

Before-Race Procedure: Begin warming up 45 minutes before the race. Do not use difficult exercises such as push-ups or sit-ups. The warm-up consists mainly of jogging and stretching. Lie down ten minutes before the race, then get up and jog a few minutes—you are now ready to go.

> TIP: A common procedure followed by many sprinters in coming to the marks is to do the "skeleton" dance, and then breathe forcefully for two or three times before getting on the marks.

Placement of Starting Blocks: The distance from the starting line at which the feet are placed depends on the height of the man. The man of average height (5' 10") locates his feet at the following measurements—front foot 22 inches and back foot 32 inches. In any case, do not crowd the starting line; be comfortable (Diagram 2).

Come to Your Mark: In coming to the blocks, the runner should back into his blocks, rather than step down. This will prevent cramps and foot injuries. In coming to the blocks, first step over with your left foot just to the front of the left starting blocks. Next step over with the right foot, and lean forward on your hands. Then back into your blocks with your left foot first, followed by the right. After this, clean the cinders from your hands.

Diagram 2

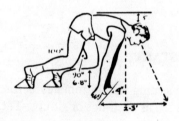

Diagram 3

Diagram 4

1. Make sure all your spikes are in contact with the starting blocks.
2. Place fingers at a high arch just behind the line.
3. Head is down looking at the ground, directly between the arms.
4. Shoulders are behind the line about 5 inches.

"Get Set" Position: Get set as shown in Diagram 3.

1. As soon as the command "get set" is given, the sprinter takes a deep breath and then holds it until the gun is fired.

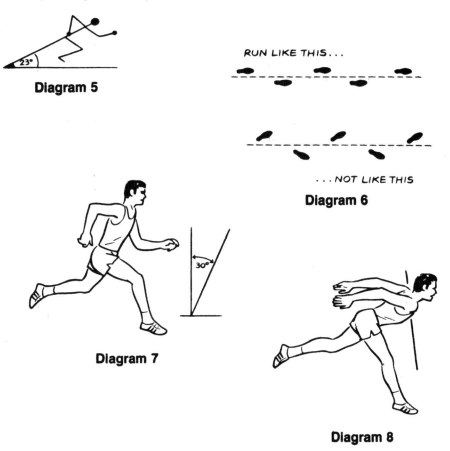

Diagram 5

RUN LIKE THIS...

...NOT LIKE THIS

Diagram 6

Diagram 7

Diagram 8

2. The head is up with the eyes focused at a spot 2-3 feet ahead of the starting line.
3. Set is assumed slowly. Weight is lifted forward, then up. Front knee is lifted only 6-8 inches off the ground. Legs are almost parallel to the ground.
4. In the rocket start, the hips are about 3 inches higher than the shoulders.
5. Weight on hands is at a minimum.

At the Firing of the Gun: Move as indicated in Diagram 4 at the firing of the gun.

1. When a sprinter leaves his marks, he should execute a vicious drive with both legs.

2. Left arm is driven long and forward.
3. Right hand is driven back only to the front of the hip and then thrust immediately forward.
4. Hands are relaxed and slightly cupped.
5. Look at the finish tape, do not look to the right or left.
6. First step is 16-19 inches over starting line, or longer if you can manage.
7. Drive out of the blocks at an angle of 23 degrees (Diagram 5).
8. Hips go forward, not up, and forward while driving off the blocks.
9. Keep feet in a straight line, don't duck-waddle coming off the blocks. Run as indicated in Diagram 6.

Running Stride: The running stride is shown in Diagram 7. For the first 20-30 yards of the race, the sprinter leans forward with all his power behind him. He runs with a high knee action; keeps hands cupped and loose; runs high on toes; runs with a 30-degree lean; runs relaxed with arms parallel to the ground. He should reach with front arm to lengthen stride; keep rear leg kick-up low; pivot from shoulder while running (see Diagram 7).

NOTE: The trained sprinter can learn through experience to run in a more relaxed manner for a few strides at the midpoint of a race. The well-trained sprinter is able to coast without loss of form and with no apparent loss of speed.

FORWARD LEAN AT TAPE

The forward lean at tape is shown in Diagram 8. About 15 yards out, take a quick gulp of air and gather mentally for the finish. Run higher on toes to lengthen stride. Talk yourself into staying loose and running faster. Keep head down and eyes on finish tape. Stay loose (jaws and hands). Never look at an opponent, or throw arms up or head back. Lean forward 2 yards out, at the hips—throw arms back, but keep your balance. Drive 10 yards beyond finish tape. Slow down gradually so you don't pull a muscle.

4

Running the Sprints

by Frank Zubovich

Assistant Track Coach
Ohio State University

Frank Zubovich has been coaching track and field on the high school and college levels since 1957. At Glenville (Cleveland, Ohio) High School, he compiled a dual meet record of 41 wins, 9 losses and 1 tie. In state competition, his squads captured the championship 3 times, and placed second twice. At present, he is assistant track coach at Ohio State University.

Sprinting is a highly individualized event, with sprinters varying in characteristics, height and weight. There is also much variance in the application of form.

TECHNIQUE: To say there is only one technique that's effective for sprinting would be foolish. However, we do utilize a basic technique, with variations occurring as demanded by physical stature or by individual preferences.

To simplify our coaching, we stress three basic parts of sprinting—the start, the run and the finish. These techniques are repeated often enough to become conditioned reflexes, requiring very little thought—and allowing concentration on such aspects as reaction to the sound of the gun, relaxation during the run and extra effort at the finish.

The Start: We favor a balanced medium start and teach it to all sprinters and hurdlers in a group. Adjustments are made as necessary during the early part of the season. Foot spacing in relation to the starting line varies with the height of the individual—the taller the boy the greater the distance between the front foot and the starting line. Usually it holds that the taller the boy, the longer the foot—and this is in keeping with the desired spacing. In inches, this comes to about 12 to 15 inches for the front foot and 31 to 34 inches for the back foot.

> SPACING: Each boy determines his own foot spacing. He does this by placing his heel just inside the starting line, and then drawing a scratch line at his toe. This is approximately where the front block is set. He then places his front foot in the block, and kneels down with his hands behind the starting line. The knee of the opposite leg is placed next to the front block—and this determines the spacing between the front and back blocks.

To proceed to the set position, the sprinter rocks forward with a steady motion until his hips are elevated to a position slightly higher than a point parallel to the track. The body moves forward until there is a slight tension on the arms which are extended straight down from the shoulders with the fingers bridging for support behind the starting line. The eyes are focused on the track a few yards in advance of the starting line. At this point, all attention should be directed to the action of the arms and legs—which will occur at the sound of the gun.

> THE GUN: On the gun, the sprinter's first reaction is a running step forward—not a lunge out of the blocks, as the novice first believes. He must drive vigorously with the arms which are bent at an angle of approximately 90 degrees at the elbow. As soon as the blocks are cleared, the sprinter strives for full extension of the driving leg during each stride—while lifting the knees as high as possible and using the arms to the fullest extent.

The Run: The angle of the runner is very acute at the first step, and increases with each stride until the desired position is reached. This position is reached after 6 to 10 strides. There is a gradual transition from starting strides to strides of full speed. With each step, the stride lengthens and the trunk angle straightens. During this portion of the race, the driving leg provides thrust by extending both the knee and the ankle. However, the knee thrust lessens as full speed is approached. From this point on, the rocking motion of the ankle becomes most important.

> RHYTHMIC ACTION: As the body moves forward, the driving leg moves backward so that the foot touches the track directly under the body. At this point, there is a strong push of the foot along with a forceful backward drive of the leg. These combined movements result in the forward movement of the body. Although using all his power, the sprinter maintains a smooth, rhythmic action all the way through the finish.

The Finish: The process of preparing for the finish is more mental than physical. About 30 yards from the finish, we tell the sprinter to prepare himself by taking a deep breath, lifting the knees a little higher and applying extra effort in the closing yards. Even though a sprinter is running at full speed, he may win or lose a race by his mental presence toward the end. There is no deceleration until the runner is 5 yards beyond the finish line.

> NOTE: Some sprinters prefer to lean for the tape at the finish of a race—and we do not discourage this if it's executed without loss of speed.

Coaching Points: In addition to having a good basic style, a sprinter must prepare himself psychologically for each specific race. He must know his own ability, assessing his strongest attributes and judging his shortcomings. If there's a weakness in one particular area, that's where increased emphasis must be placed during practice. A good sprinter not only takes stock of his own abilities, but also knows the capabilities of his competitors. Self-confidence is the primary factor for a sprinter—and it comes with work and believing in the method of training used. A knowledge of the theory and mechanics of sprinting will also aid a sprinter's self-confidence. And here, the coach must be a teacher—showing not only *how* but also *why*.

5

Tips on Sprinting Techniques

by Dr. Leroy T. Walker

Head Track Coach
North Carolina (Durham, North Carolina) Central University

Dr. Leroy T. Walker will be the head coach of the U.S. Olympic team in Montreal in 1976. The head coach at North Carolina Central for over 25 years, Dr. Walker has coached 8 Olympic medal winners, and his squads have captured numerous team individual crowns–N.A.I.A. national championship (1972), M.E.A.C. championship (1972, 1973, 1974), to name a few. Dr. Walker is the holder of numerous individual honors and the author of three books and various articles on track and field. This article is based on his work with Edwin Roberts, one of his top sprinters.

I agree that any boy can run, because running is a perfectly natural action. Sprinting in track, however, requires a technique as exact as that employed by any field event man. Thus, it's essential that the

Photo 1

coach analyze the form of each sprinter to see that he is deriving the greatest possible benefit from it.

ALL SHAPES AND SIZES: Sprinters come in all shapes and sizes—there just isn't any "ideal" body build for the sprinter. Not having a fluid-action Bobby Morrow, a strong Bob Hayes or a tall, free-swinging Ray Norton is no reason to panic. The coach must develop the material at hand. One of our top sprinters, Edwin Roberts, is a case in point.

Edwin Roberts (Photo 1) is five feet, eight inches tall and weights 158 pounds. His best sprint series are a 9.2 for the 100-yard dash and 10.1 for the 100 meters; 20.1 for the 220 yards on the straightaway; 20.3 for the 200 meters around one turn; 46.0 for 440 yards. His assets as a sprinter are a fine start, relaxation and excellent leg reflex. Here are some tips on sprinting techniques—per Edwin Roberts.

The Start: A prime prerequisite for a good start is "mental toughness" in approaching the starting line. This attitude is not suddenly generated as the sprinter waits for the gun. Roberts developed this toughness through hours of practice as he gained confidence in his own ability to start. In each starting practice, attention is given to the following details:

1. Make each gun start a separate production which approximates the conditions of an actual competitive start. No sloppy starts are permitted and recalls are made however slight the forward movement before the gun reports.

2. Concentrate on listening, not on thinking or anticipating.

3. Avoid too much pressure upon the hands and locking elbows.

4. Assume a "get-set" position which guarantees maximum momentum from the blocks—not just quickness of arms-legs coordinated action.

5. "Run up" to the best running position. The exact distance from the blocks or exact number of strides before the desired body lean for efficient running will be achieved varies from runner to runner.

6. Guard against a "planting action" of the foot that leaves the rear block.

7. Achieve maximum momentum through effortless acceleration.

> NOTE: An important phase of Robert's start is his sensitivity to the sound of the gun. He has no gimmicks with which to gain an advantage—just complete concentration. Every other possible stimulus must be shut out. The primary goal is to reduce the elapsed time between the report of the gun and the initial thrust against the starting blocks.

In the "on-the-mark" position, Roberts gets as close to the starting line as possible while maintaining proper leg position (angle for drive in both legs), a desirable hip elevation, and a generally comfortable position. He shifts his weight forward to the desired pressure on his hands while still "on-the-mark." No additional forward movement is made. This permits Roberts to make the proper hip elevation and to maintain adequate pressure against the block in the "get-set" position—a pressure which is frequently lost when the sprinter shifts his weight forward on the command "get-set."

Although the action of the first stride results in firm, explosive placement of the foot upon the track, and is accompanied by an upper-cut thrust with the arms—Robert's foot strikes the ground in his first stride from the blocks as if the track was a hot stove. The "hot-stove" action prevents the "planting" of the foot which causes the slight hesitation in those first strides—a very costly action that slows momentum.

Roberts concentrates on "running up" to his best striding position. In the initial thrust from the block, his head is kept level and directly in front of his shoulders. Once he has achieved his drive and has reached his most effective "lift point," no attempt is made to keep his head down beyond the point of no return.

EVALUATING MOMENTUM: Frequent evaluations are made of Robert's' ability to cover ten and twenty yards of the first part of the dash. Use of the stopwatch to determine the speed with which he covers these distances is a means of evaluating momentum achieved in the early strides.

Acceleration and Easy Striding: Roberts practices a continuous series of knee lifts to retain his unusual ability to accelerate with little effort. His emphasis is on fast leg reflex which he achieves through good hip and knee action. The arm thrusts are faster, but there is no corresponding speed up of upper body movements.

NOTE: It's absolutely essential to make a quick recovery in each stride. Further, the sprinter should maintain just enough forward lean of the body to permit him to drive with his feet behind him and still maintain proper balance. Every ounce of power must be generated by each leg before the foot starts up from the track in the recovery of the leg.

Roberts achieves the recovery action by quickly pulling the heel of his recovery foot toward his buttocks to avoid a "hanging" action of the leg upon completion of his drive power.

A daily routine which includes relaxed, easy-effort striding is followed to achieve the proper relaxed acceleration pattern. Thirty-yard knee lifts much higher than practiced in normal running action are performed in the daily practice schedule. The sprinter accelerates after thirty yards to get the "feel" of increased speed with a minimum of body action. This acceleration is accomplished by reducing the knee elevation and quickening the leg reflex. The fact that the knee lifts are performed at a slow speed makes the task easy.

REMEMBER: Probably the most important factor in sprinting success is the ability to relax. Relaxation and effortless acceleration save power for the final drive at the end of the race.

6

Workout Techniques for Sprinters

by Lindy Remigino

Head Track Coach
Hartford (Connecticut) High School

Lindy J. Remigino speaks with authority on sprinting. He's a champion himself: member of U.S. Olympic Track team 1952, winning 2 gold medals for the 100 meters and 400-meter relay; IC4A 220 champion (1952), 100 and 220 champion (1953); Melrose and K of C N.Y. sprint winner (1952). As head track and cross-country coach at Hartford (Connecticut) High School since 1953, he has had his share of winning seasons, which include several sectional, city and State titles.

Sprinting is the most natural form of any running event in track. So when selecting dash men for your squad, look for two things: some natural speed and body strength.

SHAPES AND SIZES: Sprinters come in all shapes and sizes. I recall running against all types—men who averaged only 130 pounds and 5 feet 4 inches in height; others who stood over 6 feet and weighed 165 pounds. Despite the great variance, these men had two important things in common—natural speed and overall muscular strength.

With these two prerequisites, here's how we apply training and workout techniques and develop winning sprinters.

Building Strength: Overall muscular strength is essential for success in the dashes. The development of strength with emphasis on conditioning the hamstrings and buttocks is most important—since these are the muscles that deliver the power in driving from the starting blocks and extending the hips and knees in acceleration.

REGULAR PROGRAM: Building muscular strength can best be accomplished by setting up a regular strength program early in the fall. The use of weights, calisthenics, and 2 to 4 miles of cross-country running are especially beneficial early in the training schedule.

Teaching the Start: We stress placing the front starting block approximately 15″ from the starting line and the rear block about 30″ from the starting line. This varies of course depending upon the length of the sprinter's legs. The sprinters should stand in front of the blocks and back into them one foot at a time.

TAKE YOUR MARK: On the "take your mark" command, the sprinter places his hands on the ground in front of the blocks—with his left foot against the front block and his right foot against the rear block. The head is lowered to relax the neck muscles and eyes are fixed on the ground just a few feet in front. Body weight is mostly forward with shoulders well over the starting line. Weight is supported by the thumb and fingers and left toe—and balanced by the right knee and toe. Arms are held perfectly straight with elbows locked.

On the command "get set," the right knee is lifted off the track just enough to place the hips a few inches above the shoulders. On the report of the gun, the sprinter drives forward, not upward, from the blocks, driving vigorously from the front block and whipping the right foot out. Keeping low for the first 15 yards enables the dash man to get into full running stride sooner

STRIDE: Naturally, the first few strides from the blocks are
going to be short—but as the sprinter accelerates, the stride
increases. The runner should learn to extend or throw from
the hips. At full running stride, it is not uncommon for the
stride to measure 76 inches.

Running Tips: Jumping upward at the start instead of driving and
running forward usually means the loss of a few important yards.
Raising the hips too high will straighten out the right knee and inhibit
good movement. Running without swaying the body from side to side
(rocking motion) and running from the hips with the knees high are
especially important tips for the 220, where relaxation is a must to
prevent the runner from tightening up at the finish.

Early-Season Workouts: Building strength takes precedence in
our early-season workouts. We warm up with calisthenics, lift
weights, and run 2 to 4 miles of cross-country daily. The dash men are
urged to run relaxed, concentrating on form. We run intervals of 220,
440 and occasionally 660 to build endurance.

Mid-Season Workouts: By mid-season, when sprinters are more
in condition, workouts are not as vigorous. So attention is now placed
on starting and speed work. Practicing starts at short distances of 35 to
50 yards is best to perfect the technique and correct faults.

TYPICAL DAY'S WORK: A typical day's work in mid-season
might include: warm-up with 880 jog; calisthenics; 6 x 150
yards at half-speed as part of the warm-up; 6 x 220 at ¾
speed for main part of the workout; jog off the workout with
an easy 880.

I don't feel that the sprinter should run all-out every day. Nor is it
necessary to practice the start under the gun each day of practice. To
my way of thinking, starts under the gun at 50 to 75 yards about 6
times per session 2 or 3 days a week are sufficient. And sprinters
running all-out every day have a tendency to pull up lame or become
stale, losing their edge.

Late-Season Workouts: This time of the year calls for tapering
off of all hard workouts. A typical day's work might run like this: jog
880; calisthenics; 6 x 160 yards at ¾ speed; 6 x 50 starts; jog easy 880
and go to the showers.

Part II

Middle Distance

1

Middle Distance Running

by Steve Bartold

Head Track Coach
St. John's (Jamaica, New York) University

Steve Bartold's 13-year record as head track coach at St. John's University is 202 wins against 109 losses. He has coached 2 Olympians (1964 and 1968); 19 NCAA All-Americans; 9 Metropolitan New York championship teams; 2 World Record holders. He was the head coach of the 1974 United States National Junior College team that beat the Russians in Austin, Texas, in 1974 and assistant coach of the United States team that competed against the USSR team in Leningrad in 1970.

The middle distance events and the development of runners to fill these spots can be considered the most important parts of a good track team. A team with winning middle distance performers is one prominent in dual and triangular meet victories, as well as in championship meets. The reason: men at the middle scale of distances can run either up or down depending upon where they are needed most in a particular meet.

QUALIFICATIONS: In order to be a good 440 man, the runner must have the speed of a sprinter and the endurance of a half-miler. He must be able to carry excellent 220 speed over 330 yards, and then have the strength to "kick" home the last 110 yards. For the 880, a boy must possess the endurance of a miler for the last 220 yards of his race. With good 440 speed, he must also be ready for any kind of first 440 yard pace the race may demand.

Our Program: At St. John's, it is part of our program to make the middle distance runner as versatile as possible, training him to cover events that are not considered his best. This versatility helps all runners and the team as a whole. Thus, workouts for the middle distance runner are varied to include events other than his own. Actual workouts are divided into three phases: early-season, mid-season and late-season. The idea is to work hard and get into shape in the early-season, and sharpen up and come to a peak during mid-season. In late-season, just hold the edge you obtained during the earlier part of the year.

WARM-UPS: The usual workout is preceded by a warm-up period for each athlete. Since some athletes require longer warm-ups than others, the warm-up period is up to the individual and the coach.

1. Early-Season Workouts: Here we do mostly distance and repeat work in the following order:

	440 Yards	**880 Yards**
MONDAY—	440's 8 to 10 starting with 68 seconds and working down to 60-62 seconds, with only 220 yards walk between.	
TUESDAY—	Repeat 660's 4 to 6 times at 1:35-1:30, walk half distance between.	Repeat 1320 yards 3 to 5 times at 3:40-3:30, walk half distance between.
WEDNESDAY—	220 yards, 4 sets of 4 about 30 seconds each, with 110 yard walk between.	330 yards, 4 sets of 4 about 32 seconds for 220, with 110 yard walk between.

THURSDAY—	Sprints, 50 to 150 yards, number governed by coach.	220 yards, 12 to 16 at 30 seconds, 110 yard walk.
FRIDAY—	880 yards, 3 times at 2:10-2:15, walk ½ distance.	1 mile, 3 times at 4:40 4:50, walk ½ distance between.
SATURDAY—	We usually reserve every open Saturday for some sort of inter-team competition. This stimulates the feeling of competition in the pre-season, and also fills the gaps in schedules during the season.	

2. Mid-Season Workouts: During the mid-season, we do less work on distance and place more emphasis on speed:

	440 Yards	**880 Yards**
MONDAY—	6 to 8 330's at 28 to 30 seconds for 220.	6 to 8 440's at 60 to 62 seconds.
TUESDAY—	500 yards, 53 to 55 seconds for 440; 440 yards at 55 to 57 seconds; 330 yards at 30 to 42 seconds; 440 yards at 57 to 60 seconds.	660 yards at 1:25 to 1:30; 440 yards at 55 to 57 seconds· 220 yards at 26 to 28 seconds; 600 yards at 1:25 to 1:30.
WEDNESDAY—	4 x 440, full rest between each, at 9/10 speed.	¾ mile at 3:10 to 3:15; 880 yards at 2:03 to 2:05; 440 yards at 57 to 60 seconds; 440 yards at 57 to 60 seconds.
THURSDAY—	Full starts at 150 yards.	5 to 6 220's at race pace.
FRIDAY—	Rest if competition on Saturday.	
SATURDAY—	Competition or inter-squad meet.	

COLLEGE LEVEL TIMES: All the times given in the above workouts are on a college level. They would be adjusted as necessary for high school athletes.

3. Late-Season Workouts: By late-season, everyone should be in good condition. Workouts now are only for the purpose of staying in condition for the remainder of the season. Here is where the big meets are being run.

	440 Yards	**880 Yards**
MONDAY—	Same workout as 880 men.	500 yards, 56 to 57 seconds for 440; 4 x 220 yards at 28 to 30 seconds; 440 yards at 56 to 57 seconds.
TUESDAY—	Starts to 150 yards; 4 x 220 yards at race pace.	660 yards at 1:25 to 1:27; 440 yards at 56 to 57 seconds; 220 yards at 26 to 27 seconds.
WEDNESDAY—	2 x 330 yards, 25 to 26 seconds for 220; rest; 2 x 330 yards, 25 to 26 seconds for 220.	3 x 330 yards, 28 to 29 seconds for 220; 3 x 330 yards, 28 to 29 seconds for 220.
THURSDAY—	Work on grass, straight-aways and pick-ups.	1 ½ miles of 110's and jog; 4 x 220 yards at race pace.
FRIDAY—	Rest for competition.	Rest for competition.
SATURDAY—	Competition.	

2

Selecting and Training the 440 Man

by Sherman B. Hall

Head Track Coach
Central (Thomasville, Georgia) High School

> *Sherman B. Hall has been coaching high school sports (football, basketball, baseball and track) for 18 years. His track squads at Central High School have won the regional championship for the past 6 years, and the state title the last 3 years. In addition to his track duties, Coach Hall serves as a consultant in physical education in high schools of Thomas County, Georgia.*

The track teams at Central (Thomasville, Georgia) High School have won the regional championship for the past six years, and have taken the state title for the past three years. The year-after-year success of the teams can be attributed to the versatility of the 440 men.

NOTE: We've won the 440-yard dash on the state level every year except one since 1961, and have established a new state record on five occasions. Since 1958, Central has been represented each year in the mile-relay in the state meet. Last year, our mile-relay team set a state record with a time of 3:28.9.

As you can see, the hero of our track team is the 440 man; he is also the nucleus of the team because of the importance placed on the other events that he may be chosen to fill. In most high school track meets the mile-relay is the last event—and often the outcome of this race determines the winner of the meet. Since the greatest pressure is placed on the shoulders of the anchor man, he must be the individual who is most dependable. Thus, the 440 man must be selected and trained with care. Here's how we go about it at Central High School.

SELECTING THE 440 MAN

Certain definite characteristics are required of the quarter-miler; however, except for the above-average height, the type of body build is unimportant. But, he must be able to run at top speed in a relaxed manner for the duration of the race. Strength and endurance are thus two vital characteristics.

NOTE: Since the 440 man is often called upon to run in other events, he must be able to recuperate rapidly after each race. This ability is often detected by a low pulse rate.

Finally, he must have a strong desire to run, because of the complexity of the training procedures and the demands placed upon the individual. Very often, potential 440 men are discovered in intramural sports and in physical education classes.

The final selection of 440 men for early-season meets is based upon performances recorded in the 330. A strong finish in the 330 indicates an ability to compete in the 880. A boy with good speed who has a weak finish in the 330 should be directed toward the 220, or possibly the distance events.

TIP: This method of selection applies more to younger, inexperienced boys than to more mature runners.

TRAINING THE 440 MAN

Although the 440 is not a form event, there are certain motions that act as corrective measures for the more experienced runner and as fundamentals for the beginner. For instance: the leg lift of the 440 man is not as pronounced as that of the runner in the shorter sprints. The continued emphasis placed upon relaxation will usually determine the length of the stride. The arm action is forward and rhythmical. Hips are not held rigid—although accentuated hip swing should be eliminated. Breathing is very natural except at the beginning and the end of the race, when oxygen intake should be more forced.

WARM-UP: Weather conditions influence the type and length of warm-up needed. Another factor to consider is the condition of the track. The emphasis placed upon the meets are both elements of consideration in warm-up procedures.

Speed: Speed is improved by a type of workout that includes short 30-, 40- and 50-yard sprints (repetitious) at maximum relaxed effort. Work on starts, with and without blocks, is necessary. Also, short bursts of speed during continuous lap-running are emphasized. A popular practice is to select 4 to 8 boys, have them maintain about a 5-yard space between each other while running around the track, and let them jog at approximately ¼ to ⅓ speed. As they continue around the track, the rear man peels off and sprints to the front of the group. When the man sprinting reaches the front of the column, the new man on the rear begins his sprint. The action is continued until all complete the workout.

Endurance: Endurance is increased by several methods. In addition to the continuous lap-running, another procedure is the division of 120 yards into three 40-yard blocks—whereby the runners jog the first 40 yards, run the second 40 yards and sprint the final 40 yards. This practice is also beneficial in insuring a better finish for the runner.

NOTE: In late season, it's desirable to relieve the runners of the monotony of running around the track by having them run on different terrain in various areas of the school campus. In warmer climates, early-morning running is preferable because less energy is expended to maintain a higher degree of condition.

In connection with the amount of running necessary for the endurance phase of the training program, caution should be taken for the prevention of shin splints by having the boys run on the grass as much as possible.

Pace Work: Pace work at 110, 220 and 330 is an absolute necessity to instill self-confidence within the boy to the extent that he himself knows best how to pace himself in a race. Pace work at these three distances must be repeated each day for a prolonged period. During this period, a series is utilized in which the individual runs 110 yards 4 times, repeat 220 yards 3 times, repeat 330 yards 2 times, repeat 220 yards 3 times, repeat 110 yards 4 times—all at a 440 pace with intervals of 5, 6, 7, and 6 minutes respectively between sets.

NOTE: Another type of practice session that includes speed, endurance and pace work is to have the boys run 4 sets (3 repetitions in each set) of 440 yards at a pace of about 12 seconds slower than their best times. There should be 1-minute intervals between repetitions and 8 minutes between sets. Each week the aim is to reduce the time by 1 second.

3

Training the Quarter Miler

by Don Kornhaus

Head Track Coach
Ottawa (Kansas) High School

Don Kornhaus' five-year record as head track coach at Ottawa (Kansas) High School is most impressive: he has won the East Kansas league championship seven years straight; the state indoor championship once (and was runner-up three times); and the state outdoor championship twice.

Over the past five years, the Ottawa (Kansas) High School track teams have seen their share of success. Although we have had some outstanding field event men, I feel that the key to this overall success lies in the ability of our boys to run a good, solid 440-yard race.

NOTE: In Kansas there are 11 running events in track and field. Of these 11, a good quarter miler can win at least nine.

Five years ago, we had only three boys who could run the 440 in less than 53 seconds. This past season, we had no less than eight who could perform this well or better. In short, I feel we produce more decent 440 men than most schools with greater enrollments. This has been the result of hard work and dedication on the part of the athletes.

PHILOSOPHY

The philosophy employed in our program can be used in any school regardless of size. It contains some of our own ideas and suggestions from well-known coaches who have had great success in track.

When school opens in September, all track men are encouraged to participate in a fall sport. I believe that a boy can help himself by competition regardless of the season or the sport.

NOTE: During the fall, boys not participating in football or cross-country are encouraged to run on their own and to lift weights.

"Long, Slow Distance" Running

The basic type of running is "long, slow distance." Here volume is the important aspect, not speed. Boys should work toward a goal of running approximately 100 miles per week. To run this distance in seven days requires extended periods of running.

The time of running exercise becomes important in order to attain heart efficiency. To develop heart efficiency, an athlete must raise his pulse rate to at least 130-140 beats per minute and maintain this rate for 30 minutes or longer.

NOTE: This can be done by long distance runs at a pace well within the ability of the runner. After each workout the athlete should be pleasantly tired but never exhausted.

Training, Not Straining: To begin long, slow distance training, an athlete is advised to run for 15 minutes in one direction, then turn back and attempt to reach his starting point in 15 minutes. At first he may not be able to get back in the amount of time allotted, but he will soon learn to pace himself.

This will mean that he is learning pace as well as forcing his body to adjust to distance running. He needs only a wrist watch to check his turn-back point. As conditioning improves, the time-out should be increased to 20 minutes and eventually reach 45 minutes.

NOTE: It is important to note that "training, not straining" is being emphasized during these early months of work.

Dedicated Runners, Only: Caution must be taken when starting a boy on the long, slow distance program. If he is really dedicated to running, then he should be encouraged. Only boys who want to work will benefit from volume running. Dedication is required because it is no fun to arise at 6:15 a.m., run from 6:30 to 7:30, shower, dress, eat breakfast, and get to school by 8:15.

NOTE: These excercises must then be repeated after school. All of this is required to be in the 100-mile-per-week club.

You may ask, "Why do all this to run 440 yards?" I can only say that I believe the quarter mile to be the one race that is most strenuous on the heart. Consider this point: the national high school record in the 220 is 20.2. Why then haven't we seen quarter milers run a 40.4 race? After all, it is only two 220's. The answer is that most quarter mile men never work for heart efficiency and in order to sprint for 440 yards, heart efficiency is necessary.

WEIGHT TRAINING

Included in our fall program is weight training. If performed properly, without straining, some endurance can be developed—but our goal is developing a strong, sound body.

We do not use heavy weights; instead our runners use light weights, performing at least 20 repetitions per exercise for three sets. Ten different exercises are used, and we lift three times per week.

NOTE: It should be noted, however, that running is never sacrificed in favor of weight training. We favor running.

OTHER WORK

At the end of the regular cross-country season all of our runners, cross-country and track, are encouraged to enter AAU cross-country meets. This provides some incentive for all runners and a meet now and then does break monotony.

During the winter, our runners work out at least four times per week. Some run seven days per week. This is a choice left to the individual. He must want to work. Our Kansas climate is not the best for winter training, but ski masks, gloves, long underwear, and heavy socks enable our boys to work out even on those days when the temperature is not the best.

NOTE: It is necessary to warn your runners often against speed work too early. They must believe in what they are doing and wait until the season starts before they attempt to bring themselves to racing form.

PRACTICE SCHEDULE

Once track season begins and regular practices are conducted, all athletes are asked to set goals for themselves week by week and for the year. Our practice schedule attempts to give each boy the opportunity to achieve his weekly goal.

As soon as weather permits, all conditioned hurdlers, sprinters, and middle distance men are asked to establish a base quarter mile. There are various methods of doing this; we use the method of former Kansas University track coach Bill Easton.

NOTE: Coach Easton's method was to have a boy run a quality 330, jog, walk a 110, and then run a 110. Adding the time for the 330 and 110 gives an indication of the athlete's potential in the 440.

It is surprising to find that most runners will be close to their base quarter time by the end of the season if the practice schedules are so planned, and if the athlete is willing to work.

DRILL PROGRAM

During the season, we utilize various drills to accomplish goals of endurance and speed for one quarter milers. We use the drills shown in Chart I.

Endurance and Speed Drills—Chart I

1. *Slow-Fast-Slow*
   A warm-up drill in straightaways using gradual acceleration for 30 yards, relaxed ¾ speed for 60 yards, and then deceleration for 30 yards.

2. *High Knee*
   A warm-up drill with emphasis placed upon a high knee lift and good arm action over 100 yards.

3. *Slow-Fast*
   Endurance work emphasizing ¼ or ½ speed over the first portion of a distance, then ¾ to ⅞ for the remainder of the distance.Usually 330 to 880 yards.

4. *Ten-Minute Drill*
   Ten minutes of continuous running with an increase or decrease in pace every 30 seconds. Speed is designated as jog, pace, sprint, then repeat by timer's signal.

5. *Four-Minute Mile*
   Running 220 yards with eight repetitions at a 28-to 30-second pace within a ten-minute period.

6. *Minute Drills*
   ¾ to full speed running for 60 seconds. On signal, jog to start and recover by using various exercises (push-ups, squat jumps, deep knee bends) then repeat.

There are many other drills that are used, but the idea is to work each boy by using a variety of exercises. If an individual does not have some pre-season work, these types of workouts must be delayed until he is in running condition. Once good running condition is achieved, emphasis is placed on quality 660's.

I personally believe that mentally, this type of running prepares a quarter miler for his goal of running 440 yards at full sprint. For us, quality over-distance running has resulted in strength, endurance, and confidence.

NOTE: Too many high school quarter mile men either run out of gas too soon, or save it too long and sprint home last. It is our goal to have quarter mile men who can run the entire race.

END-OF-SEASON PRACTICE

Toward the end of the season, early-week practices consist of a reduction in volume of running. With the league and state meets approaching, we prefer to have our runners rested, fit, and mentally prepared.

We often cut practice short, and on occasion have group swimming instead of practicing. Doing this helps morale as well as being good therapy on tired legs and good heart exercise.

CONCLUSION

It is important for the coach to remember that he is working with boys, and each boy has a longing for some success. A coach cheats a boy if he doesn't work him hard enough for some recognition. If you are fair with each boy on your team, he will not object to hard work—we have found this to be so. Remember, hard work can produce good quarter milers from average athletes who have average speed.

Coaching the 880-Yard Run

by Ed Styrna

Head Track Coach
University of Maine (Orono, Maine)

Ed Styrna has been head track coach at the University of Maine since 1956. During that period his teams have won 80 meets and lost 35. This includes six Yankee Conference titles and 10 State championships. He was assistant track coach at Dartmouth for eight years before moving to Maine.

The 880-yard run is an extremely demanding event. It calls upon the runner to have speed, endurance, a sound knowledge of pace and a good grounding in race tactics—in other words, *all* of the requisites of *all* the other running events. There is no magic formula to make a runner a champion. It takes hard work. Here is how we go about it at Maine:

Pre-Season Work: To achieve the greatest success, all half-milers should either run cross-country or run fall track practice. The type of fall track work would be similar to cross-country, but not quite as intense.

GOALS: The primary goals of any early season practice are to build endurance through overdistance running, prepare the legs for future work, and gain overall body strength.

Assuming that the half-miler doesn't choose to run cross-country, here is the type of program I would give him. I would try to get his legs ready for work by having him run 440's and 880's at a slow pace, broken up with short walks in between each run. This should be done on a grass surface. As soon as leg soreness (the most common being calf soreness) disappears, I eliminate the walking in between and make the boy run continuously at a slow pace. The distance is gradually increased until the runner is covering 5 to 6 miles. In time, the pace is increased until he can carry a strong pace over the 5 to 6 miles.

On alternate days, I have the runners do repeat speed work well above their 880 pace. I try constantly to increase the pace of these runs. We also do some fartlek.

STRENGTH: To gain general body strength, I advocate isometric exercises and am a firm believer in hill running to strengthen the legs.

Competitive Season Work: The primary goals of competitive season work are to build up speed, endurance, a good sense of pace and a sound knowledge of racing tactics.

INTERVAL TRAINING: I believe that the best single method of training runners during this phase is interval work. The factors of this type of training—distance, number of times run, pace and the time of the rest interval—can be juggled in an endless variety of ways. How they are used depends on what goal or combination of goals is the prime objective of the coach *and* what the runner needs most.

Once into the season, almost all of our training is done on the track and is timed. The distances that we use in 880 interval training are 220's, 440's and 660's. In order to vary the fare, I throw in days of wind sprints and fartlek conditioning away from the track.

In general, repeat speed work is the best way to develop wind. By its nature, it creates in the body a great oxygen debt. The body, in turn, adjusts to this greater stress and learns to create its own tolerance to the debt. All of our half-milers do a lot of speed work on 220's and 440's at a much faster than racing pace. (Assuming the case of a potential 2 minutes flat 880 man, I would give him 220's at 25 to 27 seconds and 440's at 55 to 57 seconds.)

> CAUTION: Pre-season work will build up your runner's leg strength so that speed work can be safely used. *But*, this work should be alternated with some medium and slow work. The reason: constant hard speed work tends to tear the legs down and sharply increases the chances for injury, especially if fatigue is allowed to become a factor.

In building up endurance through repeat 220's, 440's and 660's, I usually keep the rest interval constant and gradually increase the number of times that the distance is run. I *never* set an arbitrary number of times that the given distance is to be run in a workout or the rate of increase in that number in future work-outs. This is determined by the degree of difficulty the runner is having in handling each workout, how he feels, and the training load in general.

Pace: It has been pretty well established that from a physiological point of view, the most economical way to run the 880 is to run as even a race as possible. One study suggests that the first quarter of the 880 should be one second slower than the second one. The theory here is that if the first quarter is much faster than the second one, the oxygen debt will build up too rapidly and greater fatigue than necessary will result during the latter stages of the race.

In practice (competition), however, the reverse of the above idea is usually true. Almost all the first quarters in the 880, as it is run today, are two or three seconds faster than the second quarter. The tactical demands of breaking for a good position and the natural forces of competition seem to be the reasons for this.

> CONCLUSION: There is no really "best" way to run the 880. Conditions are the deciding factors. I would say that in a race where pole position was important, such as an indoor race, the expenditure of a lot of energy to get position could be justified. On the other hand, if the race does not require that the runner get pole position, I would advise the runner to stay close to the leaders and run as even a race as possible. In the typical 880 race today, the leader at the quarter-mile is usually not the winner.

I believe that the best present method of building a sense of pace in a runner is to clock him in practice over repeated fractions of his race—220, 440 and 660. During competition, he should be given his times at the different points of his race so that he will know whether or not he is maintaining his pace schedule.

THE GROOVE: The repeat nature of interval training is ideally suited for getting a runner in a certain pace groove. (In the case of our two minute half-miler, I would have him run repeat 220's in 30 seconds, 440's in 60 seconds, and 660's in 1:30.) A properly trained runner should be able to hit any one of his distances within a tolerance of five tenths of a second, plus or minus.

Tactics: The 880 is a race run at a relatively fast pace and most of it is run at close quarters. This means a lot of maneuvering for position, especially in any running done on a small indoor track. To prepare my half-milers for any eventuality, I give them the following general rules on racing tactics:

1. Make a try for the pole position at the start, but not at the expense of a sound pace plan.

2. Normally, if in the lead, you can ease off slightly on the turns. Be alert, however, for passing attempts when coming off the turns or on the straights.

3. If an opponent challenges you for the pole, pick up the pace slightly to discourage him.

4. If you don't get the pole and are running behind someone, run on his right shoulder. If someone comes up to challenge you, move out with him or you run the risk of being boxed in.

5. If you get a poor position breaking for the pole, *don't panic*, but work your way up gradually. If you are still strong yourself, it will be easier to get by runners in latter stages of the race when they are tired.

6. When passing on a small track, it is usually best to start picking up speed coming off a turn and make the attempt as you go into the straight.

7. Never pass unless you feel that you have a good chance to get by your man. Never make a half-hearted attempt. Go by your man as though there is no doubt in your mind about it—and there shouldn't be any.

8. If a man starts to ease off too much going into a turn, you can sometimes "jump" him before he regains his momentum. On the other hand, don't be lured into attempting this pass by someone who eases off just enough to let you pull up even with him, and then picks up just enough speed to run you wide around the whole turn.

Part III

The Relays

1

The Sprint Relays

by Maxie Hays

Head Track Coach
Alexandria (Louisiana) High School

In four years as head track coach at Mansfield (Louisiana) High School, Coach Hays saw his teams win the district, regional and state championships all four years: (1971–Class AA; 1972 and 1973–Class A; 1974–Class AA). He is now head track coach at Alexandria High School (Class AAAA).

In selecting runners for the relay teams—440 and 880 sprint relays—we consider the following: speed, ability to compete, ability to exchange the baton.

After we have selected the four boys to use in the relay, we give careful thought to the order in which we run them. Here, we consider best starter, strongest runner, best curve runner, best competitor for anchor man.

BATON EXCHANGE PRINCIPLES

Regardless of the method of baton exchange that you use, stick with the following basic principles:

1. Neither the incoming nor the outgoing runner should slow down during the exchange.
2. Constantly strive to have both runners traveling at top speed when the pass is actually made.
3. Do not change your method during the year. Convince the boys that your method is best suited for them.

NOTE: Our method of baton exchange is the blind-verbal exchange.

440 RELAY

Number One Man: We want our first man in the relay to be a fast starter and a strong runner. He gets down to start with the baton in his left hand, the first finger and the thumb in a spread position helping to support his weight.

NOTE: The first man runs the inside of the lane until he gets approximately halfway through the exchange zone, then he lets his momentum carry him to the outside half of the lane.

Number Two Man: The number two man stands at the back of the international exchange zone in a crouched position with the left foot back, as indicated in Diagram 1. If we have a real strong runner who can get us a lead, we put him in the number two spot and strive to put pressure on the other teams.

NOTE: He watches the incoming runner over his left shoulder and starts running when he (the incoming runner) hits the check mark. He drives off with his left foot at the angle indicated in Diagram 2.

In practice, we tell our boys constantly to be sure that the incoming runner is over the check mark, then try to run off and leave him. We want the two man to use vigorous arm and leg motion to gain speed (Diagram 3), always looking straight ahead.

When he hears the command from the incoming runner, he extends his right arm straight back, locking the elbow, with his hand

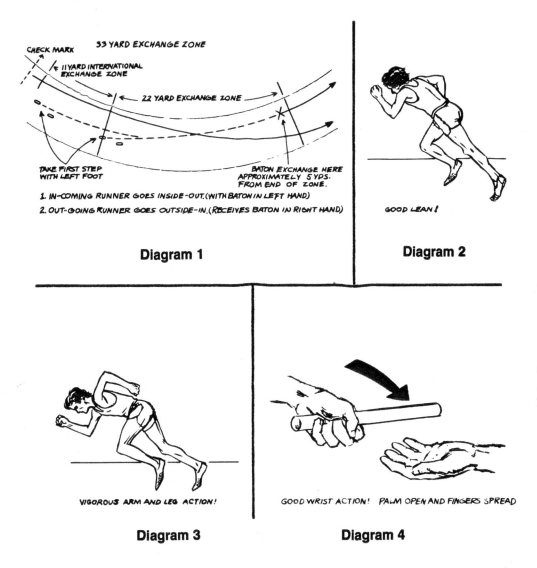

Diagram 1

Diagram 2

Diagram 3

Diagram 4

open to receive the baton (Diagram 4). He should keep his shoulders forward, the palm of his hand level, and fingers pointing at the incoming runner. His hand must be held steady.

After getting the baton, the number two man shades the inside of the lane. The incoming runner should always finish strong, running at top speed all the way through the exchange zone. The arms of both runners should be fully extended.

Number Three Man: The number three man stands at the back of the international exchange zone, in the outside half of the lane, with his left foot back and looking over his left shoulder. When the number two man hits the check mark, the number three man runs a straight line out of the exchange zone. He takes the baton in his left hand. As he nears the curve, he shades the inside of the lane, as did the number one man.

Number Four Man: The exchange with the number four man or anchor man is the same as it was with the second man.

NOTE: The first part of our practice session each day is devoted to the relay exchange. We don't place a time limit on this phase of the session—we stop when we're satisfied and then continue with the rest of the workout.

880 RELAY

Our workout procedures for the 880 relay are a little different from those for the 440 relay.

The exchanges are the same except that we don't use the international exchange zone for each man, as we do in the 440 relay.

We practice the 880 relay exchanges on those days of the week that our sprinters run 220's in their workouts. We run the full 220 for each leg at top speed all the way through the exchange zone.

NOTE: We try to use the same four boys in both relays at the same positions. We run the slowest man of the four at the third leg of each relay. These two factors give us more consistency as the season progresses.

2

Success in the Relay Events

by Ronald Johnson

Head Track Coach
Vinita (Oklahoma) High School

Ronald Johnson has been head track coach at Vinita High School for the past 15 years. During that time his teams have won 1 state crown and 7 conference championships out of the last 8 years. His teams have won over 50 team trophies. He coached Jeff Bennett who at only 5' 8" and 150 pounds became NAIA Decathelon Champion and placed fourth for the United States in the 1972 Olympics in that event.

A review of statistics indicates that during my nine-year tenure as track-and-field coach at Vinita (Oklahoma) High School, we have enjoyed relative success with two events in particular—the mile relay and the 440-yard relay.

NOTE: While it would be a gross error to state we have developed a unique program, whereby championships will always be the end result, we do feel we have utilized some fundamental concepts or techniques that have significantly contributed to our success in the relay events.

We would be happy to share our thinking with other coaches —hopefully contributing in some small way to their success.

FIRST FIELD EXERCISE

After our initial meeting with the squad, the first field exercise calls for all team members to run the open quarter under the usual practices of observation and physical discipline. A designated timer sounds the whistle at the 50-second mark and each runner's position is marked accordingly.

For purposes of clarity, let us assume that a boy's position is marked at the 420-yard point. In this instance, we inform him that he is 20 yards away from an $8,000 endowment. We impress on him that any young track man who can run the track in less than 50 seconds will have little difficulty in securing a full scholarship to a major college or university.

NOTE: We then instruct him to consult our active participant files and see for himself where our 50-second runners are now participating. It's extremely meaningful for the boy to see on paper that each of our 50-second people has been awarded a full scholarship.

50-SECOND BARRIER

Following this initial introduction to our program, the boys are given a weekly opportunity to break the 50-second barrier—the idea being for him to add 2 or 3 yards to his distance over the preceding running. It is surprising how hard a boy will try to get that last 5 or 10 yards he lacks.

NOTE: We know from experience that this technique has made 50-second quarter-milers of several 53- or 54-second men. We are of the opinion that this drill inspires the individual to exert that maximum effort in practice—and, as coaches, we are aware that this is where the track meets are actually won or lost.

The drive has enabled us to have eight or ten strong quarter-milers and, subsequently, the nucleus of a good team.

RELAY WORKOUTS

The 440-yard relay has been reasonably good to us here at Vinita. In our workouts, we start at the 110-yard marker and run to the 330-yard mark. Immediately following our conditioning drills we work for a minimum of 30 minutes on the baton exchange, having each man run only 55 yards. These sprints are always timed by one of our coaches—and the boys are shooting for the 220-yard school record.

The varsity is always in lane two; the second team in lane three; our sophomores run in lane four. Our school is small enough for us to combine the junior high and high school in drills. We normally have the freshman runner in lane five, followed by the eighth-grade and seventh-grade runners in lanes six and seven, respectively.

NOTE: When working on our baton exchanges we find that the younger boys, by being there and watching the varsity, are soon making the exchanges correctly—with our having to say very little to them. The upper-classmen will, by example, materially add to the development of the younger boys concerning all correct elements of the exchange.

OPEN 220

When running this 220-yard relay, we always put a boy in lane one and let him run the open 220 against the relay team. This is our basic teaching tool—allowing the baton men to see how they fare against the open runner.

If the boy running the open 220 grossly gains on the relay team as they make their baton exchanges, then it becomes apparent to the rest of the boys that there wasn't a good baton exchange. They therefore realize that they have to make that exchange without letting the baton ever slow them down—if they want to win the race.

NOTE: By utilizing our varsity, we believe that if we have four boys who know how to make the baton exchange, there is no reason why we couldn't have 40 boys also knowing how to make the exchange. You just put them in relay workouts for a couple of weeks and have them run and watch the varsity.

MENTAL CONDITIONING

This factor is simply one of terminology, but we think that it's most important. For instance, instead of telling a boy that he is to run ten quarters during a practice, we tell him he is to run ten "60's." This means he will be called upon to run ten times for 60 seconds at maximum effort. In other words, all that boy has to do is run ten minutes hard—and if he's worth his salt he can do that.

> NOTE: The boy will much more readily accept this conditioning practice because it doesn't appear to be the hard work of running the quarter ten times. He will adapt his mental acceptance to the time requirement much better than to the distance requirement.

FELLOWSHIP OF CHRISTIAN ATHLETICS

Our entire athletic program has been strongly motivated by attitude development resulting from participating in the local chapter of the Fellowship of Christian Athletics.

During our first meeting with the squad, we tell them something we read some time ago in a piece of F.C.A. material. The material concerns the type of boy the coach is attempting to locate.

We tell the squad, "We are looking for that boy who would run until he couldn't run any more, and then he walked—and he walked until he couldn't walk any more, and then he crawled—and he crawled until he couldn't crawl any more, and then he got up and ran again."

> NOTE: If you see a young man in your audience grin, indicating that he understands the implication, you just might be talking to the next state champion.

3

The Relay as a Springboard to Success

by Mark Cotton

Head Track Coach
Grant (Portland, Oregon) High School

Mark Cotton has been coaching track and field for 21 years, the last 13 years at Grant High School. His dual record there is 70 wins and 2 losses. His teams have won 9 district championships and 4 state championships. Coach Cotton was a member of the 1970 Olympic distance training staff at the University of Oregon.

Coaches make great efforts to persuade large numbers of boys to report for track and field, but often they do not follow through on the more difficult task of keeping boys from dropping out through lack of interest.

On our squad one motto is "Run for Fun," and the main method to achieve that enjoyable state is the relay race. I feel that the most effective means to maintain excitement and participation is the relay race, in practice and in meets.

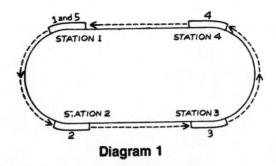

Diagram 1

NOTE: No man who comes out for track is ignored in our practice or meet relay program. There is a relay for everyone.

Breakup of Squad: What we do in practice, following the usual warmup, is divide the boys into three squads, depending on their specialties, for relay competition.

- Group 1: Shot putters, discus throwers, javelin throwers.
- Group 2: Sprinters, hurdlers, high jumpers, long jumpers, pole vaulters.
- Group 3: Middle distance and long distance men.

GROUP ONE RELAY

The coach in charge divides the boys into five-man teams, with a serious effort to even off the teams in ability so that there will be a lively sense of competition.

Using the outside lanes of the 440-yard track, the five-man teams will run from three to five continuous 440-yard relays. Each athlete runs 110 yards, passes the baton, and remains at the station until his turn comes up again (Diagram 1).

NOTE: The fifth man is placed at the first station and takes the baton from the runner who started from the fourth station. The latter rests at the first station until the relay comes around to him again.

Resting and Running: Because the presence of five men on a team enables one to rest once during five rounds of the track, it is possible to mount a continuous relay.

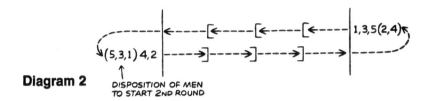

Diagram 2   DISPOSITION OF MEN
TO START 2ND ROUND

For every five rounds, an athlete runs a total of 440 yards. This gives him the speed work so essential to improvement, as well as the pleasure of the challenge by rivals.

GROUP TWO RELAY

The second group sets up a low hurdle shuttle type of relay on the infield grass, where the coach again divides his forces into teams of approximately equal ability.

The course need not be longer than 80 yards, with two lanes, and three hurdles set at 20-yard intervals in each lane (Diagram 2).

> NOTE: There must be as many such setups as there are teams. However, each team may number five or seven men to insure adequate rest in a continuous relay.

Rules for Relay: In this type of relay, the rules call for one half of the team to line up at one end of the course and the other half to line up at the other end. If the team is odd-numbered, there will be an extra man at one end and that end will start the relay.

The No. 1 man starts in one direction. When he finishes the course, he taps the No. 2 man who makes the return trip in his lane. He taps the No. 3 man and so forth, with the relay continuing as long as the coach deems necessary.

> NOTE: The less adept athletes often hit hurdles and fall but this is not injurious because the course is on grass. The football coach, for that matter, is likely to claim out the track men who go through hurdles instead of over them.

GROUP THREE RELAY

There are many relays that can be done on the inside lanes of the track and the most strenuous one is reserved for the distance men. This is the "parlauf relay."

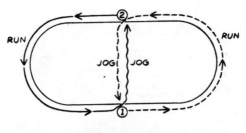

Diagram 3

This event is a two-man relay in which the starting runner goes 220 yards at a distance pace, passes the baton to his partner at center track, and jogs straight across the infield to receive the baton as his partner completes 220 yards (Diagram 3).

NOTE: The parlauf readily may be used as a pace work relay, with each runner aiming for a specific time for 220 yards, such as 35 seconds.

For Two Miles: The parlauf can be used competitively over a long distance, too. For example, a two-mile relay would require each runner to carry the baton eight times.

NOTE: The coach likely will find the boys aiming for records in this sort of racing as they gain interest.

POLICY ON RELAYS

We incorporate this relay work into two or three practices each week, with the groups changing each day to a different station.

NOTE: The tyro, or unskilled runner, has no fear of standing out in his awkwardness because everybody participates and there are boys of comparable ability on each team.

Finding Talent: Because of this rotation of the relays, we often find unused talent as the season progresses. Several years ago our top two high hurdlers were a high jumper and a pole vaulter developed in the shuttle hurdle drill.

NOTE: The distance relays uncovered distance-running talent in a member of the shot put squad.

RELAY MEETS

Every track schedule should have at least one relay meet in it. We have a "City Relays" meet in Portland for each level of competition.

NOTE: That is, we have a freshman relay meet, and others for junior varsity and varsity.

Emphasizing Teams: The idea in Portland is to emphasize the team aspects of track, with the hope that spirit will carry over throughout the season.

Entry is limited to three events per athlete, with no more than two to be running events. The coach therefore must depend on athletes in various spots who usually are not point-winners in dual meets.

NOTE: This practice often develops confidence in athletes who have not previously had the chance to show their talent. For instance, a sophomore taking a leg of the distance medley with the team stars may surpass himself to merit this assignment.

A wise coach will look for such situations to aid the runner who has not quite reached his potential. With planning, a non-placer can be given a chance to share the winning of a blue ribbon.

Value of Dope Sheet: A relay meet demands a careful evaluation of the strengths of other teams, and generally a team enjoys running down the dope sheet.

If comparisons enable the coach to show each relay unit where it should place, the boys will do their best to excel this placement.

NOTE: A coach who shares this planning with his squad not only will make track more meaningful to the boys, but also may learn things to his advantage. Boys can be a step ahead of the coach in thinking at times.

RELAYS IN DUAL MEETS

In all our dual and championship meets we have the 440 and mile relays, and these are the most important events to us because they are scored 5-0 rather than 5-3-1 for individual events.

That means that a team which can count on winning these events can count on holding its opponent at a standstill while it picks up 10 points. Obviously, this can be tantamount to winning the meet in a close contest.

Passing the Baton: Because of the importance of passing the baton in the 440-yard relay, it is wise to select this team and its alternates as early as possbile.

NOTE: This permits ample practice in a standardized method of handling the baton by runners who grow to know each other's style.

The pass in the mile relay is not so crucial and since it is the last event in the meet, it is not critical if the team championship already has been determined.

This allows a greater degree of personnel switching than in the 440, but a meet that is in doubt down to this final event demands the best men available.

NOTE: Otherwise, the mile relay offers a coach an excellent chance to measure the ability of a green man.

Whenever possible in dual meets, we like to agree with our opponents to schedule a weight man's relay. This does not enter the team score but it is a real crowd-pleaser and the weight men clamor for it.

In this event, we reiterate our original premise that participation for all must depend on the motto ''Run for Fun.''

4

Coaching the 880 Relay

by Steve Hansen

Head Track Coach
Woodland (Washington) High School

> *Steve Hansen has been coaching high school track for 15 years. As head track coach at Woodland High School, he has produced 2 state championship 880 relay teams and set a new state record. He has also seen his share of district and individual championships—two district crowns and a second place; six individual state champions.*

The running of relays is the only track event that really involves teamwork. Due to this fact, a good relay team can be of great value in uniting the entire track squad.

NOTE: The relays are the popular events on most track squads—and the popularity of relay carnivals has given added interest to relays of all kinds.

The techniques that will be discussed are the ones that have been successful for us over the past years and are responsible, in part, for our 880 relay team winning two Class "A" state championships in addition to setting a new state record.

Order of Runners: There are many thoughts on the placement of the runners in a sprint relay. At Woodland High School we like to have our best starter run the first leg of the relay. This way we can take advantage of his starting ability since, if the first man falls behind in the race, the rest of the team may become discouraged.

Our best sprinter, and one we hope will be a fierce competitor, will run the anchor leg of the relay. Whether our second man is the third or fourth best sprinter is of little concern. We place these men where they might be able to pass and receive the baton with a boy they like to work with.

TIP: If two members of the team are returning from the year before, we like to have them run in the same positions as before. The experience helps.

Method of Exchange: In the 880 relay, or in any other sprint relay, the speed of the exchange is of the utmost importance. The method described here is only one of the many methods.

The exchange is made from the left hand of the incoming runner to the right hand of the outgoing runner. The outgoing runner will have a predetermined starting line, approximately 7 yards, scratched on the track. As the incoming runner approaches this mark, the outgoing runner will drive hard as if he is coming out of the starting blocks.

NOTE: He will utilize vigorous arm action for the first 10 to 12 yards. At this time, he will extend the right arm behind him to receive the baton. The right arm must be locked at the elbow, and the wrist must be cocked forward so that the palm of the hand is down (Figure 1).

The fingers are together and the thumb is spread wide. It is very important that the elbow is locked, as this prevents movement of the arm and hand. If the receiver is approaching the end of the exchange zone, and he still doesn't have the baton, he should slow down until he receives it. He must never turn his head and shoulders to see where the incoming runner is. This turning action forces the receiving hand far out of position at a very critical time.

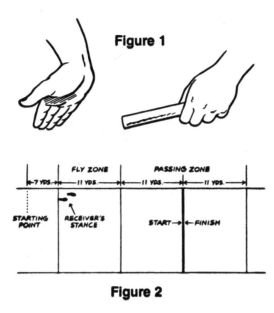

Figure 1

Figure 2

Figure 3

Techniques: When the outgoing runner takes his position inside the restraining line, he should stand facing the direction in which he will run. His feet should be placed so that the toes are pointed down the track. They should be staggered as if they were in the starting blocks. By assuming this position, the runner will be able to obtain a much faster start due to the increased ankle push possible.

> NOTE: The incoming runner will continue to drive through the exchange zone until the exchange has been completed. He should "gather" as he enters the legal passing zone (Figure 2). He should continue his normal arm action until he is ready to make the exchange. He should never run the last 8 to 10 yards with his arm extended in position to pass the baton.

The exchange is made with a snappy wrist action, not a full sweep of the arm. This wrist action is important in making a proper pass. A missed exchange with a sweeping arm action is fatal, whereas a short wrist action can be made again without a lot of wasted time and motion. The incoming runner must stay in his lane after making the exchange so that he will not foul another team.

As was mentioned earlier, the speed of the exchange is a primary objective. The "free distance" between the passer and the receiver is a distance that only the baton covers. The greater this distance, the more efficient will be the exchange. This "free distance" can only be developed through continuous and dedicated practice.

International Exchange Zone: The exchange zone is 22 yards in length: 11 yards either side of the 220-yard marker. In the past few years the International "fly" zone has been added. This gives the outgoing runner the opportunity to start an additional 11 yards closer to the incoming runner (Figure 2). The baton, however, cannot be exchanged in this area. It must still be passed in the regulation 22 yard zone.

This "fly" zone can be a valuable asset to a sprint relay team as it gives the runners involved in the exchange an extra 11 yards in which to synchronize their speeds before making the exchange. An ideal exchange is made approximately 15-18 yards into the regulation exchange zone. Thus there is a margin of safety of only two or three yards. By using the International zone, however, this safety margin can be increased to approximately 10 yards. This increased safety margin gives the runners a great deal more confidence, which is extremely important.

NOTE: An additional advantage of the zone is that it is now much easier to get the fastest man on the team to run an additional 7 or 8 yards. We like to have our third man pass the baton to our anchor man as soon as possible after entering the legal exchange zone. This way our fastest sprinter will be running approximately 228 yards instead of 218 to 220 yards. This technique works with any of the exchanges.

Starting with the Baton: The lead-off runner on a sprint relay is confronted with the problem of holding the baton while positioning himself in the starting blocks. The official track rules state that the baton cannot touch the ground in front of the starting line. We have found that, with practice, this problem of keeping the baton off the ground is easily solved. This rule is not often enforced in dual competition, but it should be observed.

The starter should hold the baton in his left hand, as he will be making the exchange with this hand. The baton should be gripped at the end so that it will be in position for the exchange. The index finger should be wrapped around the baton, thus holding it securely against the base of the thumb. The starter's weight will then be supported by his thumb, and the middle, ring, and small fingers (Figure 3).

WHERE TO FIND RELAY MEMBERS: The four top sprinters on the track team will generally make up the sprint relay team. However, in a small high school the coach may have only two sprinters. Other members of the track team who may be potential relay members are the long jumpers, the pole vaulters, or the hurdlers.

Training Relay Members: The members of the relay team will get their conditioning work in their regular events. Therefore, specific training methods will not be discussed here.

The training of the relay squad as a whole is devoted to handling the baton. The members of the team should work on their handoffs at least three days a week. At the beginning of each workout period, the handoffs should be practiced at half speed to facilitate the handling of the baton. At Woodland we never run time trials in the 880 relay. We do run 440 relays for time occasionally. When doing this we time each 220, thus getting motivated competition between the first two runners and the last two runners.

One method of working on handoffs is the use of the "parlauf relay." We use this to get additional conditioning work, or in place of endurance work on a particular day. Parlauf relays can be run in many different ways, but we use the 440 relay with four runners, our relay team. The lead-off runner will cover 110 yards and pass the baton to the second man, who will continue the relay. The first runner, after handing off, must jog back to his original position and wait for the anchor man to finish the 440 and pass the baton to start the second relay.

Each other member of the relay team likewise jogs back to his original position for the second, third, and fourth turns. These relays are not run at full speed. The entire relay should be run in approximately 58 to 60 seconds. To maintain this time over a series of relays, the runners must run faster as they get tired. A single workout may include 8 to 10 440's. With this method we get practice in exchanging the baton as well as conditioning work.

NOTE: When working on full-speed exchanges we work two exchanges at the same time. The first man passes to the second man while the third man passes to the anchor man. We feel that by practicing this way in the same exchange zone we get more realistic experience. The second man also follows this procedure.

5

Coaching the Relay Exchanges

by Bobby Wicker

Head Track Coach
Lee (Baton Rouge, Louisiana) High School

> *In 12 years as head track and field coach at Lee High School, Bobby Wicker has compiled a record of 98 wins against 22 losses. This includes 9 district championships, 2 regional championships, 2 state championships.*

All things being equal, we believe that every boy who comes out for track is a relay runner, regardless of size, height, or other considerations. We have had winning relay teams with boys 5′ 6″ tall, 135 pounds to boys 6′ 2″ tall and 210 pounds. With this in mind, we start locating our track team through relay running.

NOTE: It's important to note that our relays are not permanent; a boy may challenge any other member once a week (on a given day chosen by the coach) for his place on the up-coming week's relay. This type of challenge has been most successful in our program. Never has a boy quit the

team because he was defeated in a challenge race
—usually, the same boy will be working to regain his place
the very next week.

This is why the work on our relay exchanges is tedious and never-ending. But it pays off in big dividends when a runner hurts a leg or is sick, for then we can insert a new boy and not worry about losing time—or possibly the race.

NOTE: We also know that, mathematically speaking, there is that main course meal of 36 big points for the normal three relay races in most high school track meets. The individual events which may yield first through fifth places may end up just being dessert.

Coaching Ideas: We are not concerned here with the workout schedule (type of running, distance, and so forth) we use for our relay teams—but rather with how we work on relay exchanges. We have found our particular methods successful for the past seven years, which have yielded five district championships and two state crowns. Every year all three relay teams have qualified for the state meet finals.

Normally, there are three basic relays run in our state meet in Louisiana—the 440 relay (¼ mile), the 880 relay (½ mile), and the mile relay. For simplicity, we call the 440 and 880 relays "sprint relays" and the mile relay the "animal's relay."

Selecting and Placing Personnel: We feel that the key to relay racing is the selection and placement of runners. In choosing personnel we use the following reasoning:

1. The number 1 man must be the best block man.
2. Our number 2 man must be a strong curve runner.
3. In the number 3 spot we want the runner with guts.
4. The fastest sprinter on the squad is the number 4 man.

The speed and timing of these four men in passing the "stick" with minimum loss of time is what we strive for in producing championship relay teams. We have seen our runners go into an exchange zone three yards or more behind, and come out of the next exchange three yards ahead. We have also witnessed teams with faster personnel lose a race to us merely on poor exchanges.

Types of Exchanges: Basically, there are two types of relay exchanges: blind and visual. We prefer blind exchange over the visual.

We use the same exchange for the 880 relay even though the exchange may not be made on the curve. However, since most of the time the same boys run the 880 and the 440, we would rather teach just one exchange.

Our mile relay exchange is a semi-visual exchange because of the incoming man being fatigued after running the 440 dash. But we still hand off left to right, right to left, etc. Because of repetition, we'll cover only one of the three exchanges. The 440 relay will be discussed since it's the shortest race and requires much more time to perfect and has less room for error.

Points to Remember: Once the outgoing runner starts to move, it's up to the incoming runner to see that the stick reaches the outgoing runner (with the right take-off marks being used by both runners).

We never change hands with the stick once it is received; it slows the runner and may also increase his chances of losing the baton. Our handoffs are made from left to right, right to left, left to right. The thinking here is that in the sprint relay the number one runner is handing off on the curve and his speed into the curve will swing him outside at the time of the exchange. The second exchange is a straight-away exchange, and the third is the same as number one.

> NOTE: Figure 1a shows the position of the first exchange man before the incoming runner reaches take-off mark. Note that the outgoing runner is in a crouched position with toes parallel on the outside line of lane. There is a slight body lean toward the direction of the incoming runner. On take-off mark, the outgoing runner explodes as shown in Figure 1b. All other exchanges are the same.

The outgoing runner swings his body forward and sprints as fast as possible away from the incoming runner as soon as the latter hits the mark that has been calculated to make the exchange. He never looks back, and he takes the baton blind. The palm of the hand is down, the elbow is slightly rigid and the thumb forms a ''V'' with the palm facing down. The thumb will face toward the inside of the track. The hand goes down only after the outgoing runner takes seven good strides ahead (Figure 2).

The incoming sprinter extends his left arm and, with an upswing motion, places the baton very firmly in the number two runner's palm. The runners should stay two arm-lengths apart. This is continued

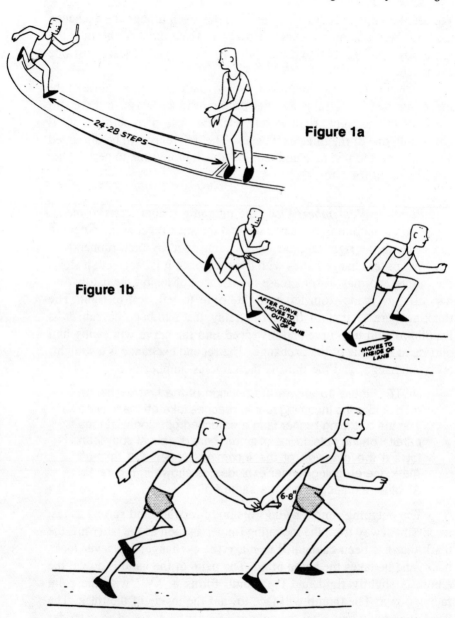

Figure 1a

Figure 1b

Figure 2

throughout the next two exchanges. The incoming runner in each case should have to reach for the outgoing runner a little—but under no circumstances should he be allowed to run up on the outgoing runner.

> NOTE: I have seen more sticks dropped this way than by the incoming man stretching a little. This little stretch will substitute a small amount of error for speed.

Summary: There's a lot of work involved in coaching the relay exchanges. It means work, work, and work. It also takes patience (mistakes will be made at first). A boy's attitude toward repetition and hard work will have much to do with his success. Some speed must be sacrificed for team unity. Also, the competitive spirit of each relay unit will many times dictate its success.

6

Baton-Handling Skills in the 440 Relay

by Jerry Martin

Head Track Coach
Eastern (Cheney) Washington State College

In three years as head track coach at Eastern (Cheney) Washington State College, Jerry Martin has won two District I and one Area I N.A.I.A. Coach-of-the-Year awards. Last year, with a squad of just 17 athletes, Coach Martin led his team to an outstanding 10th place finish in the N.A.I.A. national championship meet.

The 440 relay has been adopted recently by many western states to replace the 880 relay. Successful execution of this crowd-pleasing race, however, requires more practice and greater coordination than the 880.

NOTE: Successful relay racing should be a focal point in building team morale and a source of pride for the team. It's an important part of building the team concept in a basically individual sport.

At Eastern Washington, all our preparation with the sprint relay team is aimed at success in the conference meet. To accomplish this, we've adopted several techniques that we feel have helped develop good relay teams.

EMPHASIS ON BATON-HANDLING

We put great emphasis on the technique of passing the baton, and play down the importance of speed in building good relay teams. Obviously, we want our fastest people on the relay team, but a runner who can't exchange the baton properly may not be on our team, regardless of his speed.

NOTE: All athletes on the squad who have the speed and baton-handling skills to be on the relay team should practice these skills, including hurdlers and quarter-milers.

We may have as many as three relay teams practicing at any given time. There are two reasons for this:

1. We have a trained replacement ready if someone is injured or ill.
2. We consider relay practice a part of the runner's daily workout, not something he does after he completes his workout. In this way, we hope to eliminate errors that may be caused by fatigue.

We use a "blind" and silent method of exchanging the baton. This technique requires great coordination between the runners.

NOTE: My experience has been that relay teams make errors when a group of runners come into the exchange zone at the same time and there are a number of verbal commands that sound the same.

SELECTION OF PERSONNEL

The Lead-Off Runner must be the type of person who is excellent out of the blocks, but he must also be the type who will not false-start your team right out of a race. Many times a poorer baton-handler can be put at lead-off. He must be an excellent curve runner, however.

The Number-Two Runner must be a fine baton-handler and have great acceleration on the straightaway. If possible, find a runner who is

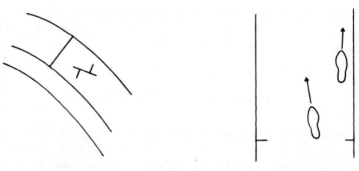

Figure 1   **Figure 2**

not completely right-hand dominant, since he starts with his left foot back and receives the baton with his left hand.

The Number-Three Runner must also be an excellent baton handler. He should be a good curve runner. He must be very competitive in case his team is behind. A good third runner can compensate for mistakes by the second and fourth runners.

NOTE: The third man should be able to pass and receive the baton in a crowd, since the staggered starting positions begin to even out the race by the time he comes into action.

The Anchor Man on a relay team must have good judgment, as well as speed and competitiveness. He should have great acceleration over a short straightaway. A less capable baton-passer can be used. Judgment in starting at the right time is important—he must not be influenced by other runners, thus starting too early and running out of the legal exchange zone.

EXCHANGING THE BATON:
LANE POSITION AND FOOT PLACEMENT

The lead-off runner starts with the baton in his right hand, gripping it between thumb and index finger, at or about its middle.

His blocks should be set at an angle to his lane. (See Figure 1.) This will assist his acceleration when starting on the curve.

NOTE: The lead-off runner should concentrate on running as close to the inside of the lane as he can, since he passes the baton to the second runner's left hand.

The second runner takes his position to receive the baton by placing his right foot as close as possible to the outside of his lane, with his left foot back and turned slightly to the center for balance. (See Figure 2.)

His feet should be at a comfortable width, with the weight on the front foot. The heel of his back (left) foot should be about 1 inch from the 11-yard run-in mark.

The second runner has his knees bent and his waist slightly forward. He looks over his left shoulder. His left arm is forward, bent at the elbow; his right arm is back, to facilitate the quickest possible start.

NOTE: When he starts, he runs as close as possible to the outside of his lane, looking at it as he runs. When he receives the baton, he runs in the center until he passes to the third runner.

The third runner takes his position on the extreme inside of his lane, with his right foot back. His left arm is back, the right forward. Both arms are bent at the elbow.

The third runner's foot position relative to the track is a mirror image of the second runner's, as is his body position.

The third runner looks over his right shoulder until the incoming man hits the check-mark. He then runs as close as he can to the inside of his lane, looking at it to stay on track. He continues to run as close as possible to the line after receiving the baton.

The anchor man employs the same techniques as the second runner.

EXCHANGING THE BATON:
RESPONSIBILITIES AND HAND POSITION

The incoming runner must run at full speed, with the attitude that he is going to run through his teammate. At about 20 yards away, he starts to concentrate on the exchange hand of the outgoing runner.

As the outgoing runner starts, the incoming runner adjusts his arm-action rhythm so that his baton hand is coming forward when the outgoing man's exchange hand is coming back.

When the baton is passed, it is placed into the hand from a running motion. It is never slapped down from higher than the regular arm action.

NOTE: We tell our runners to stab with the baton, not slap.
The incoming runner can't run full-speed with the baton held

in front for several seconds, nor with it held higher than the normal action.

The outgoing runner can only judge when to start if he has practiced repeatedly with the incoming man. He must learn to judge the speed and acceleration of his partner through daily practice.

NOTE: We use tape on the track to establish a check-mark. When this has been done, the distance is measured so it can be marked off on other tracks. Runners must be aware that check-marks will change as the season progresses and runners reach their maximum speeds.

The outgoing runner must run full speed away from the incoming runner. As he reaches back for the baton, he doesn't bend and his hand is never raised higher than his hip. He never violates proper running form.

When the receiving hand is brought back, the thumb is at about a 90-degree angle from the index finger; the fingers are spread. The baton is placed in the hand at an angle so the thumb and fingers can grasp it easily.

NOTE: The hand must be held still, without bouncing. The incoming runner puts the baton in the hand; the outgoing runner must pull it out of his teammate's hand.

If the outgoing runner does not receive the baton when he reaches, he must slow down slightly and keep his hand in the same position. This will allow the incoming runner to place it properly.

All exchanges should be made at arm's length. This saves valuable time.

TIMING THE REACH

In the early season there is more chance for error on the reach, due to less practice. We tell our outgoing runner to reach as he crosses the line making the back end of the exchange zone. This allows adequate time to compensate for errors.

As we move into the season, we delay the reach until the outgoing runner attains full speed. But he *must* reach by the middle of the zone.

BATON-HANDLING DRILLS

1. Standing Pass. Team members work in pairs, passing to the runners to whom they'll pass in actual races (one to two, two to three, etc.). They stand in place and move their arms in a running motion, each watching his partner's hand.

EMPHASIS: Quick hand action; keeping baton low; stabbing with it.

2. Train Drill. Relay men jog slowly around track in reverse order of start. Each coordinates his arm action with his partner's in front of him.

EMPHASIS: Quick hand; baton low; stabbing with baton.

3. Zone Drill. All team members work in one zone and take turns working on proper foot and body position. Two lead-off runners bring the baton in to two number-two runners, who then bring it to two number-three runners, and so on.

Runners vary their speed from half to full, over appropriate distances.

EMPHASIS: Footwork; handwork; body position.

4. Hard at the Pass. This drill is to work on timing the outgoing runner's takeoff. All runners get in their exchange zones. The incoming runner runs 40 yards at full speed and continues through the exchange zone.

The outgoing runner takes off at full speed and runs hard through the exchange zone, then eases to a jog until he gets to 40 yards from the next runner. Then he runs full speed again.

NOTE: This drill can be repeated six or seven times before fatigue begins to reduce its effectiveness. The coach should view the exchanges from a high vantage point.

Part IV

The Hurdles

1

Selecting and Developing the High School Hurdler

by Nate Long

Former Head Track Coach
South (Salt Lake City, Utah) High School

Before turning to coaching in 1936, Nate Long was a track man in his own right—receiving All-American ratings in the 440. As head track coach at South (Salt Lake City, Utah) High School, he has guided his squads to 14 city and regional championships and 5 state championships. He has also produced 4 individual "all-around champions," the most coveted track award in the state. Coach Long is a frequent lecturer at Track Coaching Clinics. He is now retired from active coaching, but has assisted at the University of Utah in recent years.

For some reason—lack of knowledge, interest or material—too many high school coaches neglect the hurdle events. Hurdling is one of the most spectacular and interesting events of the track and field program. It's a form event which demands exactness in timing and rhythm. With a little work and patience, it can be taught.

NOTE: Besides all this, we can't overlook the fact that the hurdle events contribute the same meet points as the other events.

Here are some ideas and techniques for selecting and developing the high school hurdler. They have helped me over the years and may be some help to you.

Qualifications: The hurdle prospect should possess, ideally, the speed of a sprinter, endurance of a quarter miler, spring of a jumper and unlimited courage. He should have reasonable flexibility, agility and coordination. Height is an advantage as it is in most events. However, lack of it can largely be overcome by speed, agility and spring.

AGGRESSIVENESS AND DESIRE: The hurdler must have the courage of a boxer—who when knocked down must get up and try again. The hurdler without desire should not be out for track—at least not for the hurdles.

Teaching the Beginner: If we assume that the hurdle prospect has had no previous coaching or knowledge of hurdling, there are at least two ways of starting the novice.

1. Have the hurdler walk up to the hurdle, lift the lead leg and dip, step over the hurdle and pull the trail-leg through. After this simple process is mastered, the sequence is speeded up.

2. The other approach is to allow the athlete to run over the hurdle in his most natural fashion—and then correct the gross and obvious errors one at a time until the desired form is achieved.

NOTE: We prefer the first method and start this training routine during the winter months whenever possible.

Common Errors: Here are some common errors to watch for and correct when teaching the beginner:

1. The hop is caused by a lack of flexibility, a fear of hitting the hurdle, or a lack of timing and coordination.

2. A faulty trail leg comes about by the toe being pointed down, knee being pointed up, and by taking a short first step.

3. Any arm action is faulty that results in a twisting of the shoulders, that causes the hand and forearm to be brought up and behind the back, or when both arms are too high and in a swinging fashion.

4. Lead-leg curve is caused by the beginner thrusting the lead leg toward the hurdle in arc-like fashion, which produces wasted motion and time.

Good Hurdling Form Analysis: Good hurdling form requires rhythm, coordination and a sense of timing. It will show the hurdler running, not jumping over the hurdle. Some special points include:

1. The hurdler should take off approximately 7 feet from the hurdle and land about 4 feet beyond it. This is known as the flight arch.

2. There should be a proper lean over the hurdle; the body should not be in an upright position.

3. The proper landing with the lead leg is to come down sprinting. The lead foot should be snapped down sharply to avoid "sailing" over the hurdle, which adds time to the race.

NOTE: As the lead leg is snapped it comes downward and backward in a running motion to enable the runner to make his stride after each hurdle.

4. There should be a long first stride. It's the only way to get in stride and continue in stride.

5. Maintain smooth arm action as in sprinting or running.

Training Routine: Early season training and conditioning should be similar to that of a sprinter or quarter miler. In fact, it's a good policy and a time-saver to have them work together on light running, starts, longer sprints and baton passing. During this stage of the training program the hurdler will learn to run, stressing the same fundamentals and form as the sprinters.

Drills and Exercises: We use the following drills and special exercises to help develop good form in hurdling:

1. Step over hurdle (middle)—stress toe up, straight ahead body action, and proper arm action.

2. One-step side hurdle (stand at side of hurdle)—stress above fundamentals.

3. Running one-half hurdle—if athlete leads with left leg, he runs down the left side of a flight of hurdles.

NOTE: This is an excellent drill for developing stride (start easy and increase speed). Also good for developing trail-leg technique.

4. Hip circle—athlete supports himself against a wall using his hand on his trail-leg side. He then moves the trail leg through the hurdling pattern. Also perform hip circle using hurdle.

5. Stand at side of hurdle—place leg and foot on hurdle, lean forward and alternate touching ground with left and right hands.

6. Quick-step hurdling—set up several hurdles and run through using short but very quick steps.

7. High hurdle stride (low hurdles)—set up several low hurdles and run through with high hurdle stride. This is very good for developing speed on highs.

8. Sitting drill—sit in "over the hurdle" position with chest, arms and lead leg forward and the trailing leg flexed behind.

TECHNIQUE EVENT: Hurdling is a technique event and good techniques come hard. It takes time and patience on the part of the athlete and the coach.

2

Coaching the Beginning Hurdler

by Woody Turner

Supervisor of Health, Safety, Physical Education and Athletics
Byrd (Shreveport, Louisiana) High School

> *Woody Turner has left active coaching but leaves behind a most impressive coaching record. In 25 years, his teams have compiled 14 state championships, 15 city championships and 16 district championships. Coach Turner has received various awards for his contribution to high school track and field. He is a frequent lecturer at coaching clinics and is past Secretary-Treasurer of the Louisiana High School Coaches Association.*

Hurdling is one of the most interesting high school track events to coach—and one of the most satisfying for the young athlete once he has perfected it to a reasonable degree. While any boy can clear a hurdle with a minimum of training, it takes constant practice to develop above-average skill.

STARTING FROM SCRATCH: I start from scratch with raw
material and teach about 300 boys a year to hurdle. Prior to
attempting this event, of course, all boys must have had
some background in the basics of running.

Here's our four-phase procedure for teaching beginners to hurdle
at Byrd High School.

BEGINNING PHASE

● Set up five flights of five low hurdles (30″) on the grass 10
yards apart, allowing 15 yards to the first hurdle.

● Demonstrate and have the boys perform some of the basic
hurdling exercises—such as the hurdle stretch on the ground, hurdle
stretch on the hurdle, leg and crotch extension on the hurdle, etc.

● Have an experienced boy demonstrate the correct method of
clearing a hurdle (Figure 1). Let all candidates practice this method on
the five flights of hurdles, as you watch and correct defects in fundamentals.

EMPHASIS: In this practice, stress stepping beyond the ver-
tical rod of the hurdle with the lead foot, and bringing the
drag leg up with knee at about 45⁰ angle and started first in
the movement. Stress also that the foot of the drag leg must
be parallel to the top of the hurdle.

● After the boys have mastered this technique, have them do the
skip step over the hurdle (Figure 2). When the lead foot strikes the
ground, the hurdler simply takes a short skip step with this foot
—which helps in regaining balance.

● Stress driving the lead leg up in a straight line and snapping it
down when clearing the hurdle. The drag leg must be brought flat at
the knee area and parallel to the hurdle—stretching out on landing.

NOTE: Most beginners will land the drag foot too close to the
lead foot placement—thus preventing the usual three strides
between hurdles. Figure 3 illustrates an aid in this respect.
Draw a line in the middle of the hurdle lane, marking right
foot and left foot placement. This will assure the proper landing for both feet.

● Now have all the boys run the hurdles, but do not stress technique at this point. As soon as they can clear a flight of five hurdles, time

Figure 1

KEEP
ON TOES

LF

RF

Figure 2

SKIP STEP

Figure 3

RF   LF

each boy. This serves as a motivating element for the next teaching session.

INTERMEDIATE PHASE

• Start this phase with the usual warm-up drills and stretching exercises for hurdling. The same teaching methods are followed as in the beginning phase, except the boys practice on a full flight of hurdles.

• Set up a full flight of low hurdles (30″), allowing 15 yards to the first hurdle. Distances between hurdles are: 23 feet for the 10-11 age group; 26 feet for the 12-13 age group; 9 yards for the 14 and above age group.

• Have the boys practice going over five hurdles—with emphasis on getting three strides between hurdles.

PRACTICE: With practice, most of the boys will have little trouble with their strides. You will also note that good form starts to develop and a marked improvement in their time.

ADVANCED PHASE

The 14-15 age group make up the advanced phase of our program. These boys have advanced from the lower brackets and have improved their time from 20 seconds for the 120-yard high hurdles to 15.6 seconds. We condition these boys to the intermediate hurdles (36″), using the following procedure:

• Set up hurdles, allowing 15 yards to the first hurdle.

• Start these boys at low hurdle height (30″) before going to the intermediate height (36″), with a 9-yard spacing between hurdles.

• As soon as they can maintain three strides with a 9-yard spacing, move the third, fourth and fifth hurdle back to a 10-yard spacing—just a few inches at a time.

• Move the first hurdle up to the intermediate height (36″) and have the boys practice clearing it from the starting line.

• Next move the second hurdle to the low hurdle height (30″) with a 9-yard spacing. As the hurdler continues to run the first and second hurdles in these positions and at these distances, you gradually move back the second hurdle to the 10-yard spacing.

● When hurdlers are able to maintain three strides between hurdles at this pattern, you set the second hurdle at the same height as the first—intermediate height (36″) with a 9-yard spacing between hurdles.

● Next, keep hurdles at the intermediate height, but with a 10-yard spacing between hurdles.

FINAL PHASE

● Set the first and second hurdles at the intermediate height (36″), with a 9-yard spacing between hurdles—and the third hurdle at the low height (30″), with a 9-yard spacing.

> NOTE: When the boys can clear these hurdles and maintain three strides between them, move the next five hurdles in the same pattern. Repeat this several times before spacing the hurdles 10 yards apart.

● Now have the boys run through a complete flight of 120-yard intermediate hurdles with a 9-yard spacing.

● You are now ready to move the hurdles to the high school, high hurdle height (39″). Begin this phase by setting the first hurdle at 39″, the second hurdle at 36″, with a 9-yard spacing, repeating the same pattern as with the 36″ and the 30″ heights. Repeat this several times before setting all hurdles at 39″ with a 10-yard spacing.

3

Developing a Hurdler

by Dean Benson

Head Track Coach
Medford (Oregon) High School

Dean Benson has been head track and field coach at Medford (Oregon) High School for the past 17 years. During that time, his teams have placed in the top 5 at state championship meets 9 of the last 14 years, and have won the conference championship 7 times. He has coached 13 hurdler finalists in state meets.

To be a winning hurdler, a boy must have or develop flexibility, strength, speed, endurance and skill to get over the barriers. A large order, maybe, but we've been quite successful at developing excellent hurdlers over the years. Here's the way we go about the job at Medford High School:

Flexibility: To develop flexibility, we use a number of exercises in our warm-up designed to increase or maintain the range of joints and muscles used in hurdling skills. The following are some examples:

1. *Position:* Stand erect, feet apart, toes straight ahead, hands on hips. *Action:* Sway trunk from left to right. The pull is felt on the inside of the thighs. (1-3 minutes each night.)

2. *Position:* Crossed legs, heels on ground. *Action:* Touch toes several times. Reverse legs and repeat. This is a good tendon stretcher for back of calf and thigh.

3. *Position:* Similar to #2 except no crossed legs. Work with a partner. *Action:* Bend at waist, arms folded, knees locked. Partner pushes gently on back of neck and bounces the upper torso of exerciser (2-3 times, 30 seconds each.) Good for loosening up back and back of legs. See Figure 1.

4. *Position:* Take mock hurdling position on ground, lead leg's toes pointed, knee not locked but slightly bent. Knee of trail leg at right angle to lead leg, heel against buttocks. *Action:* Go through hurdling dive vigorously with proper arm and dive action. See Figure 2.

5. *Position:* Lie on back and spread arms. *Action:* Bring left foot to right hand, and right foot to left hand. (Repeat 10-20 times each warm-up.)

6. *Position:* Take bicycling position upside down, high on shoulders, feet straight over head. *Action:* Drop lead leg to hurdling position and bring trail leg to side at 90° angle. Then pull back to original position; all action is vigorous. Good exercise for developing snap over hurdle without losing forward lean. (3-5 minutes in warm-up.)

7. *Position:* Set hurdle to high-hurdle height, and place trail leg on hurdle in trail leg position. *Action:* Bounce and touch toes with fingers, knuckles and palms. This loosens groin and pulls on lead leg tendons. Reverse procedure and put lead leg in trial leg position. See Figure 3.

8. *Position:* Place lead leg heel on left top of hurdle. *Action:* Lean forward in dive position, using proper arm action. Rock down on lead leg several times.

9. *Position:* Jogging. *Action:* Bring lead leg up to take-off position and dive with upper body. Snap lead leg down. Use proper arm action; hold lean after snap-down and point toes. Good exercise to correct many faults. We take 3 to 5 steps between exercise and repeat 10 to 15 times.

Strength: Many of our hurdlers use weight training during the off-season, but we do not make it mandatory. During the winter and spring training we work on the following strength exercises:

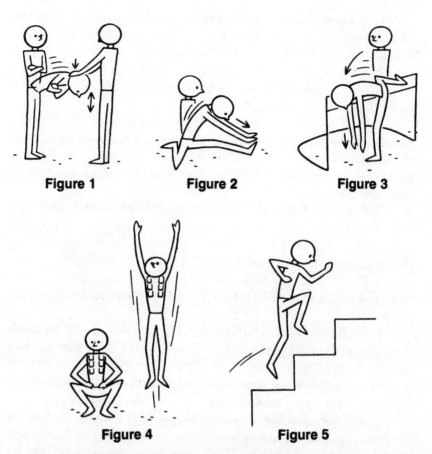

Figure 1   Figure 2   Figure 3

Figure 4   Figure 5

1. *High-knee running in place*. Bring knees as high as possible and as quickly as possible. After 10 seconds, lean and stride out 15 to 20 yards. Repeat 10 to 12 times.

2. *Ankle flips*. Run with stiff locked knees and pointed toes at ¾ speed. We do 50 yards, 6 to 10 times.

3. *Hopping on one leg*. 10 yards right leg and 10 yards left leg. Repeat 10 times using running action form.

4. *Jump squats*. Using a 10 to 20-pound weight jacket, from squatting position leap as high as possible from both legs. See Figure 4. It's good to do this exercise with a starting gun for reaction.

5. *Running of grandstand stairs*. Concentrate on leg speed, high-knee action, arm action and running on toes. See Figure 5.

Speed: We find that with strength comes speed. We emphasize strength exercises 1, 2, 4, and 5 for developing speed. Correct running form (lean, high-knee action, arm action, high on toes, etc.) is stressed in form-running workouts. These are usually repeat 110's and 220's on the grass, run at ¾ speed.

ONE POINT OF EMPHASIS: A boy works on one point of emphasis at a time until all the elements of running form are mastered to the best of his ability.

We also have our boys run "lines" on both corners and straight-aways to help straighten out feet. From time to time, our hurdlers work "starts" with the sprinters, usually with a hurdle in their lane. These are run in groups of two or three making it easier to pick out faults.

Endurance: Our typical hurdle work starts with 15 to 20 minutes of flexibility exercises, 30 to 60 minutes of sprint work—and then the endurance work for 15 to 30 minutes. We strive to keep this section of the program from becoming monotonous by varying each workout.

EXAMPLE: We do repeat 110 build-ups on grass, start easy and build to 7/8 speed at 55 yards out and full effort from there; repeat 220's, 1/3 build-up, 1/3 stride, last 1/3 build-up again; repeat starts over 3 hurdles, then sprint the rest of the race at 120 or 180 yards; continous relays for 5 minutes.

Skill: Most aspiring hurdlers have a certain amount of skill or "style" for the event; it just needs correct development. In this re-spect, body type, innate ability and even the personality of the boy all play their part. Working on form does most to correct individual faults and style. In our form workouts, we use 2 to 3 hurdles and starting blocks. The boys spend 5 to 15 minutes side hurdling, working on trail leg and maintenance of lean. After the side hurdling, everything is full speed from the blocks for 25 to 60 minutes.

MAJOR FAULTS: The major faults of most high school hur-dlers stem from the dive and arm action. To develop a good dive and lean over the hurdle, we have our boys reach below their knees and dip their heads. Or we put a towel about 2 feet in front of the hurdle and have the boy watch and reach for the towel as he dives over the hurdle. To correct arm action, we check the lead leg for bent knee and pointed toe, and work on keeping the elbows close to the body and bent following the snap down.

During the form period, we also have timed runs with 2 runners in a heat. These runs are never full distance (high hurdles, 60-90 yards;

low hurdles, 80-140 yards; sometimes just the curve). They help build confidence, pick out faults and improve finishes in a race situation.

Year-Round Schedule: If our hurdlers do not participate in other sports during the off-season, we keep them on a year-round schedule. In the fall, we work on strength and endurance with weight training and cross-country. The winter months are spent in weight training and hurdling in the gym. In the summer, we run a complete all-comers program with twice-a-week workouts and clinics. Also in the summer, junior high school boys start hurdling. So by the time a hurdler reaches high school, he is fairly well versed on fundamentals, and our job then is to do our best to make him a winner.

4

Sprinting Through the Hurdles

by Dr. Martin Pushkin

Assistant Professor of Health and Physical Education
Virginia Polytechnic (Blacksburg, Virginia) Institute

> *Dr. Martin Pushkin had only one losing season in ten years of coaching track and cross country at VPI. His teams won 30 of the last 32 dual meets in track and field and his hurdle teams have always been outstanding. At present, he is a full-time assistant professor of health and physical education.*

There are many qualities which a first-rate hurdler must develop through his endless hours of determined and conscientious training. These qualities include balance, relaxation, rhythm, quickness, and speed. Each plays a significant role in the total process of hurdling, and one quality should not be disregarded at the expense of the other. However, this author is of the firm conviction that speed is the most necessary of the above-mentioned ingredients for a top-flight hurdler.

NOTE: Quality hurdling demands quality sprinting, and the hurdler should always be trained as a sprinter. His workouts should always focus on speed and speed development. This article will be concluded with several examples of the type of workouts recommended to develop quality hurdlers, but at this point it is imperative that we review the basic components of hurdling.

Hurdling can be evaluated and studied in terms of starting, approach to the hurdle, lead-leg thrust, body pitch, trail-leg action, cutdown, and recovery. Head alignment, shoulder alignment, and arm carry will also be discussed in terms of their relation to overall efficiency. Special emphasis will be placed upon speed and its importance in the total hurdling process.

STARTING

The procedure for starting in a hurdle race is not unlike that procedure followed in the sprints. The placing of the blocks is relative to the height and leg length of the athlete. It is important, however, that special care is taken to assure that the athlete's front leg while in the blocks is flexed sufficiently to allow adequate extension at the start. At the "mark" position it is recommended that the hurdler roll slightly forward over the hands, which are directly in line with the shoulders. This premature rolling forward will prevent the athlete from having to rock forward at the set position and will prevent many false starts.

At the "set" position, the hips should be raised to a height which is as near as possible to normal hip position while running. The lead leg at the set position should be flexed at 90° to allow maximum extension at the start. The arms should be slightly bent at the elbow to allow quick reaction. Special care should be taken to prevent the athlete from locking the elbows while at the set position. An elbow which is locked will not react as quickly as one which is not locked, and it is very important that the arms aid the athlete in driving out of the blocks.

NOTE: The first few steps out of the blocks should be quick and explosive. Leg-and-arm speed are of primary importance at the start and throughout the entire race. The athlete should constantly be reminded to "think fast" and always to think of himself as a sprinter and not just a hurdler.

APPROACH TO HURDLE

The athlete should develop the ability not to overanticipate the first hurdle. Concentration at the start should be directed to the start and not to the impending hurdle. There should be no difference between running the first 15 yards of a hurdle race and an equal distance in the sprints. Through concentrated effort involving repeated runs at the first hurdle, the necessary blending of speed with control can be accomplished.

LEAD-LEG THRUST

The lead leg should be thrust just above the center of the hurdle. Having a definite spot at which to direct the foot of the lead leg will give the hurdler purpose and will aid in his concentration. Purposeless hurdling is not efficient hurdling, and this holds true for practice as well as for meets.

NOTE: Every effort should be made by the hurdler to lead with the knee of the lead leg. The lead leg should be straightened, but not fully extended, so that the cut-down will be facilitated and the hurdler will recover on a slightly flexed leg.

BODY PITCH

Body pitch can best be accomplished by trying to drive through rather than over the hurdle. The last step before leaving the ground should be shortened slightly. This will shift the center of gravity forward and prevent the hurdler from floating over the hurdle. The shortened last step will enable the hurdler to obtain the all-important pitch as the split is made, which complements forward lean and low clearance which is so necessary to efficient hurdling. The hurdler should be reminded always to attack or charge the hurdle.

TRAIL-LEG ACTION

The trail leg is an important but often neglected ingredient to quality hurdling. The trail leg represents the runner's step to the next hurdle. It must be pulled through with force and purposeful direction.

The toe is everted and the foot is positioned directly behind the knee. The knee is pulled through high under the armpit and up into the chest. This motion is complemented by a quick and powerful cut-down of the lead leg. The trail-leg action must not be carried out too quickly, as this will bring about poor balance when running off the hurdle.

CUT-DOWN AND RECOVERY

A rapid and powerful cut-down is necessary in order to achieve a fast recovery off the hurdle. The quicker the cut-down, the faster the athlete will be able to reach the next hurdle. As the foot of the lead leg touches the ground, the pressure should be applied down and back to facilitate extension, which is imperative to good sprinting.

GENERAL CONSIDERATIONS

The head and the eyes are the key to proper body position. As the hurdle is approached, the eyes concentrate on the top center of the hurdle. Remember, it is this part of the hurdle at which the lead leg is thrust. As the first hurdle is cleared, the eyes focus on the next hurdle, and this method is followed for each succeeding hurdle.

The shoulder should remain square to the hurdle. The drive of the upper body stems from the arms and not from the shoulders. The arms should be carried about waist high and kept relatively close to the body. The arms should aid in body lean and balance, and special attention should be given to sprinting-arm action between the hurdles.

COACHING AND TRAINING TIPS

1. At least 20 minutes of each practice session should be allotted to stretching exercises, which include ground hurdling, crotch stretching, hip circles, and lead- and trail-leg exercises.

2. At least 15 minutes should be spent running easy over the side of the hurdles. This type of warm-up will improve body pitch, lean, and trail-leg action. The runner should emphasize quickness, and the trail leg should be pulled through high and close to the body.

3. Have your runner kick his lead leg to a spot on the wall. The lead leg is very important as it establishes flight arc.

4. Sprinting intervals (without hurdles) should always be at least 60 yards to allow maximum acceleration.

5. Always talk fast times and get your athlete to think about quickness.

6. Time your runner to the first hurdle and between hurdles to evaluate his acceleration or lack of acceleration.

7. Ninety-five per cent of all workouts should be done over the hurdles. Back-to-back intervals over the hurdles will build strength and speed.

CONCLUSION

The 120 high hurdler probably has a maximum potential of between 12.5 and 13.0 seconds. This time will be run by an individual who can "put it all together." It will require the proper blending of speed, balance, rhythm, and relaxation. Of these ingredients, speed is probably the most essential. For this reason, great emphasis should be placed upon speed development. This can best be accomplished by sprinting workouts complemented by a well-controlled weight program.

The most successful hurdlers are men who "sprint through the hurdles."

RECOMMENDED SCHEDULE

Chart I-Competitive Season

Monday

  a. 20-minute warm-up, including jogging and stretching.
  b. 10-15 minutes of running over side of hurdles.
  c. 4 x 110 yards (running start) sprints—walk-back recovery.
  d. 1 x (8 hurdles)—walk-back recovery.
  e. 2 x 60 yards from block—walk-back recovery.
  f. 1 x (6 hurdles)—walk-back recovery.
  g. 2 x 60 yards from blocks—walk-back recovery.
  h. 2 x (3 hurdles); walk-back recovery.
  i. 2 x 330 at 3-5 seconds over best 330 time.
  j. Warm-down.

Tuesday

  a. Usual warm-up.
  b. 10-15 minutes running over the side of hurdles.

   c. 1 x (10 hurdles) at 5-minute interval.
   d. 1 x (8 hurdles) at 5-minute interval.
   e. 1 x (6 hurdles); walk and jog a 440.
   f. 4 x 120 yards (from the blocks); walk-back recovery.
   g. 2 x 220 at 25-26 seconds; walk 220 interval.
   h. Warm-down.
   i. Weight training.

Wednesday

   a. Usual warm-up.
   b. 10-15 minutes running over side of hurdles.
   c. 1 x (6 hurdles); walk-back recovery.
   d. 1 x (4 hurdles); walk-back recovery.
   e. 3 x (3 hurdles); walk-back recovery.
   f. 3 x 60 yards (from the blocks); walk-back recovery.
   g. 4 x 150 yards sprints—walk-back recovery.
   h. Warm-down.

Thursday

   a. Usual warm-up.
   b. 10-15 minutes running over side of hurdles.
   c. 3 x (3 hurdles); walk-back recovery.
   d. 3 x (2 hurdles); walk-back recovery.
   e. 4 x (150-yard sprints).
   f. Warm-down.
   g. Weight training.

Friday

   a. Easy jogging and general loosening up.

Saturday

   a. Competition.

Sunday

   a. Easy jogging.
   b. Loosening-up day.

5

Drills for Hurdling Success

by Jack Keller

Head Track Coach
Dayton (Kentucky) High School

Jack Keller has been head track coach at Dayton (Kentucky) High School for five years. His teams were Class A regional champions and state runners-up in 1972, regional champions in 1974, and finished third in the state meet in 1973. His hurdlers have dominated the northern Kentucky region; in ten regional final hurdle races (5 high, 5 low), his hurdlers have captured seven firsts, four seconds, and three thirds. Two of these regional winners went on to take state titles.

There are no magic secrets in the drills described here. The purpose of each drill is to put more interest and competition into daily practice. The drills will not cut down the amount or intensity of the work needed by the athlete or his coach, but they will decrease the chances that this work will become boring and too repetitious.

SHUTTLE HURDLE DRILL

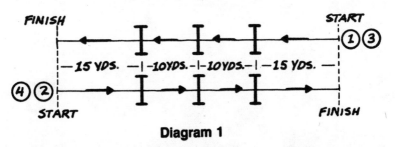

Diagram 1

NOTE: While always an advantage, excellent facilities and equipment are not necessary to produce good hurdlers. We don't have a track, and much of our hurdle practice is conducted on concrete. Furthermore, we never had more than 14 hurdles—half of which were made in the school shop.

SHUTTLE HURDLE DRILL

For this drill (Diagram 1) we use six hurdles placed at the regular distance, with three facing in each direction, as in the "shuttle hurdle relays" run at many relay meets. We divide the hurdlers into two teams of three or four each. Team A runs the hurdles as in a shuttle hurdle relay and team B then runs trying to beat team A's time. Since the boys put out more effort if the teams' times are close, we pair up the teams as evenly as possible.

Variations: A good variation is to use six hurdles and have the teams actually race against each other. For further variation, use four or five hurdles instead of three. However, we stick to three for several reasons: three hurdles can be repeated for several repetitions without the boys tiring too quickly; younger hurdlers spend a great deal of practice time working with three from the block, so this is a natural carry-over; the weaker hurdlers can only handle three in the beginning and still maintain any degree of form; three hurdles give the boys plenty of practice on their steps between hurdles and on form, while being short enough that the start comes into play.

NOTE: Two hurdles do not give enough form work since the hurdler is still using the momentum built up in the 15-yard sprint from the start to the first hurdle.

We keep records for best individual and team performances. Such records provide new team goals to shoot at and also allow the individual to compare himself at various stages of the season to some of our former champions. This first drill develops hurdling under pressure, encourages hurdlers to run for time, and is a good starting drill (each runner goes from the blocks).

TRIAL LEG DRILL

Here, the hurdler sprints in a cleared lane alongside a flight of hurdles and whips his trail leg over each hurdle as he passes. We usually start with low or intermediate hurdles rather than high hurdles. But boys with good flexibility can progress to the high hurdles. This drill is excellent for teaching proper trail leg snap and high knee lift, so important for good hurdling.

NOTE: The drill can also be used as a warm-up after stretching exercises. When used for warm-up purposes, we use low hurdles, at least in the beginning, and have the boys jog beside the hurdles rather than sprint.

We often use this drill as a shuttle hurdle relay, with the boys simply whipping over the trail leg instead of going over the hurdles. As in the first drill, individual and team times are recorded and new best efforts recognized.

OVER-DISTANCE HURDLING

This drill is a good conditioner for the hurdlers who do not run in other events or in relays. It is also good for the boy who tends to tighten up over the last couple of hurdles or who loses concentration when tired or when faced with good competition.

We use 11 or 12 hurdles for this drill, and have gone to as many as 16 for certain individuals. It's most important not to use so many hurdles that the boy tires and his form comes completely apart near the finish. When this happens, the drill is defeating its purpose of keeping the boy from "coming apart" near the end of the race.

NOTE: Each individual must be considered separately in selecting the number of hurdles he should try to handle in the drill. In pre-season or early-season practice, fewer than ten hurdles might be "over-distance hurdling" for many boys.

And for some unskilled hurdlers, unfortunately, this might be true throughout the year.

Variations: There are many variations to help make this drill fun and interesting: (1) *Timed Trial*. In this variation, all hurdlers are timed over a designated number of hurdles (the number does not have to be ten or over; you can establish squad records for 11, 12, etc.). Times of certain hurdlers can be added together for team times, and new combinations can be shuffled to take a crack at the team record.

NOTE: This team idea really keeps all the boys, not just the stars, interested. New records are usually rewarded with fewer 220's or some other workout distance repeats than the other hurdlers must do.

(2) *Overdistance Shuttle Hurdles*. This drill can be incorporated with the first drill, if you have the space and the necessary hurdles (we don't). However, we have executed this drill on several ocassions when we were practicing at other schools' tracks. (3) *Decreasing Distance Drill*. The team or individual is given a certain time to beat—say, 12 hurdles. If this time is broken, the next repetition is over fewer hurdles. If an individual or team breaks the time on three repetitions in a row, they are finished practicing for the day.

NOTE: We have had very good success with this version of the drill. We announce that the boys must do three repetitions over three hurdles, for example. Then we add that when each time we set as a goal is equalled or beaten, we'll cut down the number of hurdles. If three times are beaten or equalled, the individuals or teams involved are excused from some other work we had planned to do.

CONCLUSION

As stated earlier, the purpose of all these drills is to make hurdle practice fun and interesting while still working on the weaknesses of the hurdlers involved. It is very important to guard against boredom in practice. Boredom leads to sloppy execution and staleness.

We have found that the few drills described in this article keep the boys interested and the competition the drills provide helps to bring out a good effort.

Part V

Distance Running

1

Motivating the Miler

by Roger V. Hoy

Former Head Track Coach
Wilcox (Santa Clara, California) High School

> *Roger V. Hoy left coaching in 1966—but also left some impressive marks in track and field coaching. While at St. Ignatius (San Francisco, California) High School, his teams were rated among the top in northern California. He had nine 880 men all running under 2:03—five of them were under two minutes flat. At Wilcox High School, one of his runners, Mike Ryan, set a national freshman record in the mile with a 4:25.5 (1961). The following year saw this same runner set a national 2-mile soph record in 9:21.3. At present, Roger Hoy is in guidance work at Wilcox.*

Training for the mile run is no lark. It takes hard work by coach and runner (and plenty of it!) to produce winning milers. The practice schedule is grueling, almost a torture.

Some boys are self-motivators. There is something in their physical and mental makeup that drives them. For the most part, however, high school boys who come out for track are average runners with average desire to practice and win.

AVERAGE NOT ENOUGH: Coaches everywhere agree that the mile run is an event that requires the utmost of physical and mental coordination and condition. They also agree that only an outstanding athlete can truly excel in the mile.

Don't get me wrong about "average" boys. Remember, it is the coach's job (yours and mine) to turn 'average" into 'outstanding." Player motivation and a tough practice schedule are the *musts*. Here is what we do at Wilcox:

PLAYER MOTIVATION

To get maximum player output, you must give your men a definite goal to aim for. It must be one that both coach and player feel is realistic. A goal isn't enough, however. You must also provide your boys with constant, visual proof of progress. Following are three motivational aids which we use at Wilcox. They are, with the exception of our practice schedule, the most important factors in our success.

The Goal: The goal you give your runners must be tangible. And the only tangible goal a coach can give is time and distance. We give this to our runners at the beginning of the season. We make sure that the time is realistic enough so as not to discourage the runner, but tough enough so that he has to work hard to attain it. Most years, our goal has been a 4:30 mile.

There is another, more intangible, goal that we use. By occasional praise and comment, we get our runners to take pride in increasing their coordination, stamina and so on as the season progresses.

NUMBER ONE: By using this goal, we get our boys to realize that they do not have to be the number one runner in order to be important or successful. A 4:35 mile is just as important to a boy who ran 5:15 at the beginning of the season as a state championship is to one who ran 4:30.

Publicity: Still another way to motivate runners is by giving them a little publicity, such as keeping a bulletin board of improvements posted in the dressing room or the school's main board.

THE LOCAL PAPER: Local papers can also help with the publicity. After every meet, or outstanding practice, we send the boys' times to the papers. If they get published, they go on the bulletin board.

A word of warning: The bulletin board can lose its effectiveness if the coach fails to post *every* boy's time. You might think that this would take an army of timekeepers. It does. But we have found that parents, teachers, local college students and non-competing teammates are more than willing to do the job.

Player Perspective: We all know that not every boy can be a winner. The trouble is that the boys don't look at it that way. And unless a boy can get the proper perspective, he's in for a big letdown. In order to prevent this, we tell each boy from the beginning of the season that all we want and expect of him is his best. We repeat and repeat this throughout the season until they are convinced of it. We never give any of our boys a chance to use this as an excuse. If we feel a boy hasn't given his all, we tell him so—in no uncertain words. We tell the boys that the only time they have the right to feel let down is when they know they could have given more.

PRACTICE SCHEDULE

Motivation of his runners is only half the coach's job. He must provide them with a practice schedule that can really get them physically ''ready'' for the mile. Here is the practice schedule we use at Wilcox. We vary the starting times according to the physical limitations of our runners.

SEASON GOAL—*Below 4:30 mile*

First day:

1. Jog four or five 440's to warm up.
2. Take calisthenics with team (10 to 15 minutes).
3. Run three 1320's. Pace set at 78 seconds for each 440. Allow 20-minute rest between each 1320. (Drop 2 seconds from the lap time and 1 minute from the rest time each week.)
4. Warm down by jogging three to six 440's.

Second day:
(1 and 2 same as above.)

3. Run eight 220's. Pace for each at 32 seconds. Rest 4 minutes between each 220. (Drop ½ second from pace time and 15 seconds from the rest time each week.)
4. Warm down by jogging three to six laps (440's).

Third day:
(1 and 2 same as above.)

3. Run four 880's. Pace set at 72 seconds for each 440. Rest 15 minutes between each 880. (Drop 1 second from the lap time and 1 minute from the rest time each week.)
4. Warm down by jogging three to six laps.

Fourth day:
(1 and 2 same as above.)

3. Run five 440's. Pace each at 65 seconds. Rest 6 minutes between each. (Drop 1 second from the lap time and 30 seconds from the rest time each week.)
4. Warm down by jogging five to seven laps.

Fifth day:
(1 and 2 same as above.)

3. Run 7 to 10 miles. For example, to a beach, park, hills, and so on.

2

Training the High School Distance Man

by Leon Johnson

Head Track Coach
De Ridder (Louisiana) High School

Leon Johnson started coaching track and field in 1965 at Opelousas (Louisiana) High School. In 1970 he became head coach there. Since then his teams have won 4 district championships and 2 state championships, and never lost a dual, triangular or quadrangular meet. He just recently became head coach at De Ridder High School.

Training for the distance races involves a year-round program, starting with the proper phase of training and then gradually progressing through several phases.

POTENTIAL: First, potential must be discovered. Research suggests that inherent endurance might be discovered by having an untrained individual run 880 yards. If he can do it in 2:30 minutes or faster, he demonstrates a certain native endurance.

Once these individuals with potential are isolated from the masses, you can then start developing the potential you discovered.

NECESSARY COMPONENTS

Before a coach can plan for the training of any event, he must first break it down into the components necessary for successful performance. This requires a detailed analysis. The next step is to set up a long-range training program for the athlete that will develop each component part.

For distance running, as most coaches will agree, the following phases must be developed—although not necessarily in this order.

1. Endurance—aerobic.
2. Stamina—strength and power.
3. Speed endurance—anaerobic.
4. Speed.
5. Technique.
6. Pace judgment.

ENDURANCE

Arthur Lydiard, the famous New Zealand distance coach, and in my opinion the finest distance coach in the world, clearly stresses two important points.

1. You must develop one aspect of a distance runner at a time and only move to the next phase of development when the runner is ready.
2. There must be a proper balance between aerobic (endurance) and anaerobic training (speed endurance).

Training in the first phase for distance running must be aerobic —for if this phase is not developed sufficiently, the potential of the athlete is limited. Aerobic training is best done through long-distance or marathon running. For this, fit the athlete with the best running shoe made; one that does not cut the heel, and that has a soft spongy heel cushion and good arch supports is the best.

NOTE: The first objective in aerobic training is to concentrate on the volume of running. The greater the volume, the higher the level of aerobic condition. When an athlete between the ages of 14 and 18 can run from one to one-and-a-half hours without stopping, he then moves to the second objective of aerobic training—developing the ability to run these long distances at a steady pace. The pace should be slightly under his maximum steady pace.

STAMINA

Mr. Lydiard believes that a minimum of 100 miles a week is necessary to accomplish this level of training (endurance at a steady pace). When a runner can do this, he is ready to move to the next phase—the development of stamina.

We use a variety of ways to develop stamina: (1) hill work; (2) running rough cross-country terrain; (3) light-weight work; (4) running stadium steps; (5) long fartleks.

NOTE: When you have developed in the athlete the ability to run long distances at a steady pace, with the stamina to master rough terrain or unexpected racing tactics, you are ready to move into the third phase of training—speed endurance or anaerobic conditioning.

SPEED ENDURANCE

Many coaches have a tendency to over-emphasize this phase of the training early and thus sacrifice the full potential of the runner for early wins and fast times. A second mistake is to unbalance the training by too much anaerobic running and not enough aerobic training. This actually destroys the program, because too much anaerobic training runs the body down physiologically.

NOTE: We feel that four or five weeks of anaerobic training just prior to the competitive season will bring sufficient development anaerobically, which will then enable you to move into the speed phase of training.

Basically, anaerobic training consists of interval and repetition work. I will not take the time here to elaborate on these aspects of training. There are any number of good books on the subjects. Also during this phase, a number of time trials are conducted at different distances to discover weaknesses in the individual's training program.

SPEED

The speed phase of training a distance runner incorporates sprinting short distances of 40 to 160 yards, with complete rest between each sprint. Stress relaxation and mechanics in this sprint training.

NOTE: We believe that once aerobic and anaerobic condition is established prior to the competitive season, this condition can be maintained for four to six weeks by just doing speed training and racing once a week.

TECHNIQUE DEVELOPMENT

Mechanics or technique development is incorporated into all phases of training. The following points should be stressed to all runners —and constantly impressed upon the younger runners:

1. Run in an upright position.
2. Keep your hips forward for a long stride.
3. Relax—constantly work for relaxation.

PACE JUDGMENT

Last, but far from the least important, is pace judgment. Both the coach and the athlete are important here.

Athletes must learn to run the race at a pace that will allow them to run the fastest, most even pace over the entire distance, and put them at the finish line completely exhausted. In other words, the runner must learn to give his all.

NOTE: As a coach, you must control the speed and pace in practice so that the runner reaches his highest "speed tone" for his most important race. For example, progress the race slowly, evenly, and don't allow the boy to run too fast too early.

CONCLUSION

Physical development is great, but it can't be achieved if the mental development is neglected or under-emphasized. The athlete must be motivated to run.

3

A New Look at Distance Running

by James Demo

Head Track Coach
Roger Bacon (Cincinnati, Ohio) High School

James Demo has been coaching track since 1965. At Glenville (Cleveland, Ohio) High School, his teams won four consecutive state championships. At Purcell (Cincinnati, Ohio) High School, his team took the Greater Cincinnati championship. Since 1973, James Demo has been at Roger Bacon High School. This article is based on his work at Glenville High School.

Glenville High School has had a strong tradition for developing championship track teams built around outstanding sprinters. Thus, up until the past few years, distance running was relegated to a minor role in the eyes of the athletes.

NOTE: Our first job was one of giving the distance men a new image. One step in this direction was to develop our philosophy of distance running.

We knew that our track athletes were top flight competitors—that they had the guts to fight it out with the best of competition at the finish of any race. But our problem was to get our distance runners in good position during the race.

NOTE: This brings us to the most important point in our thinking on distance running—we want our distance men to be front runners.

FRONT RUNNER PHILOSOPHY

Too often we had seen a boy who could have run a good race completely give up at the end of a distance event because he had let himself fall too far behind. We stress keeping our runners in the race as long as possible—believing that a runner will put out more effort when he's in the thick of the competition.

Being a front runner has many advantages. As we said, if you have a runner who is a real competitor, put him out in front and then let him "gut" out the final part of his race.

We found that a front runner who sets a hard pace at the beginning of a race will have a good chance of killing off the runner who tries to hang on and then finish hard at the end.

The front runner will be more consistent because he does not have to rely on someone else to run the race for him.

NOTE: The man who runs just hard enough to stay with the pack and then tries to kick it in at the finish gains nothing against poor competition because he loafs most of his race.

SCHEDULE FOR DISTANCE MEN

Our distance men all run their races on a schedule. Each runner has his own schedule as to his event and his ability. We tell all our half milers, milers, and two milers to run the first 220 yards of their race as hard as they can without tightening up.

TIP: This relaxed sprint will put us in or near the lead, more often than not.

From here on each runner knows what time he should be on or

under for each quarter mile of his race. We also try to give our half milers a 660-yard time for which to strive. We want our runners to get the first part of their race down to time. Any improvement in total time should come in the last part of their race.

EXAMPLE: For example, if we have a miler who we think is capable of running a 4:20 mile by the end of the season, we might make out his schedule as follows: quarter mile time: .58 seconds; half mile time: 2:05; three-quarter mile time: 3:12; then the best you can get, we tell him.

The first time out he will probably run a very poor last quarter mile. However, if he can hit his first three-quarter mile time, then as the season progresses he will get stronger and his last quarter mile will improve. Also, if the runner is a good competitor, he will not want to lose the race in the final lap.

NOTE: We set our first quarter mile time low enough so that we figure we will have the lead at this point.

TRAINING PROGRAM

To achieve full success from this style of running, the distance men must be familiar with the thinking behind being a front runner. You, as the coach, must sell your men on the idea that this is the best way to run the race. Once this is accomplished, you can then help the runners through a specially designed training program.

We strive to make our distance training interesting and challenging, and try to put the greatest amount of work in the shortest amount of time. We find we can get the most out of our athletes through a series of short, hard sprints—which accomplish two important points in our program:

1. They get the runner used to running at a faster pace than he will actually run in his race.
2. They help the runner get used to getting out fast in the beginning part of the race.

NOTE: The speed work proved successful enough—but we had to resort to two-a-day workouts to get enough training accomplished.

MORNING WORKOUTS

For our morning workouts we go with strictly over-distance work. The main objective here is to develop the runner's strength and work toward a smooth, relaxed stride.

To keep this from becoming tedious, we take our distance runners off the track and send them out on cross-country type runs through a nearby park. We start out with runs of 2 miles at the beginning of the season and work up to runs of 5 or 6 miles at the end of the season.

AFTERNOON WORKOUTS

In the afternoon workouts, we run our distance men in two groups based on ability. The first group consists of our top runners and the second group of the less experienced runners. Since less experienced men become more discouraged working with the top runners, they can accomplish more by working with runners of their own ability.

NOTE: Both groups run the same workout and try to hit the same times. One group runs while the other group rests. The speed work-outs for our distance men consist of running repeat 150's, 220's, 330's, 440's, and 660's at near top speed. Sometimes we jog between each and other times we walk. A typical work-out schedule is shown in Chart I.

Our basic plan is this—a relatively light workout Monday; our hardest workouts Tuesday and Wednesday; ease up a little on Thursday; then a really good warm-up on Friday. We stress a good warm-up for our distance men, and have a prescribed set of stretching exercises. We also believe in a cooling-off period at the end of practice.

GUIDELINES

In brief, our distance program follows these guidelines:

1. Find the boy who likes to run and will work hard to succeed.
2. Stress the importance of a good warm-up.
3. Two-a-day workouts are necessary to get the most out of a distance runner. If a boy is good by working out once a day, he can become better by working out twice a day.
4. Train the distance man to be a front runner. Give the runner a steady diet of speed work. He must feel that the pace he is running in a race is always too slow.

5. Set up a schedule of lap times for the runners. Concentrate on getting the first part of the race down to the proper time.
6. Have runners of near equal ability working together when possible.

Chart 1

Typical Workout Schedule

MONDAY A.M.

Warm-up
Stride 3 miles in park
Showers

MONDAY P.M.

Jog 2 laps
Warm-up
Stride: 10 - 50's ¾ speed
10 - 220's all must be under 29 sec., 4 min. rest between each
Jog 2 laps - - - Showers

TUESDAY A.M.

Warm-up
Stride 4 miles in park
Showers

TUESDAY P.M.

Jog 2 laps
Warm-up
Stride: 10 - 50's ¾ speed
10 - 220's all must be under 30 sec., 220 jog between each
Jog 2 laps - - - Showers

WEDNESDAY A.M.

Warm-up
Stride 4 miles in park
Showers

WEDNESDAY P.M.

Jog 2 laps
Warm-up
Stride: 10 - 50's ¾ speed
10 - 440's all must be under 60 sec., 5 min. rest between each
Jog 2 laps - - - Showers

THURSDAY A.M.

Warm-up
Stride 3 miles
Showers

THURSDAY P.M.

Jog 2 laps
Warm-up
Stride: 10 - 50's ¾ speed
8 - 330's all must be under 40 sec., 4 min. rest between each
Jog 2 laps - - - Showers

FRIDAY A.M.

No workout

FRIDAY P.M.

Jog 2 laps
Warm-up
Stride: 10 - 50's ¾ speed
12 - 150's all must be under 19 sec. Walk back to start
Jog 2 laps - - - Showers

4

Conditioning the Distance Runner

by Larry McClung

Head Track Coach
Shelby (Montana) High School

Larry McClung is head track coach (since 1968) and head cross-country coach (since 1967) at Shelby (Montana) High School. In track, he has won two state championships and three divisional titles. In cross-country, he has won two state championships. He was named Coach-of-the-Year in 1968 and 1969 by the Montana Coaches Association.

For the last three years, we at Shelby (Montana) High School have been quite successful with our track and cross-country programs. This success has come about not because we have had a great deal more talent than other schools, but because of our conditioning program.

NOTE: I feel that one of the keys to conditioning is discipline. Most coaches have good training ideas and techniques, but getting the athletes to conform to these ideas and techniques is another story.

I certainly agree that each athlete reacts differently, and that the coach should take these variations into consideration—but I also believe that when discipline is needed, it should be meted out.

PHILOSOPHY

I look for two qualities in distance runners before I spend much time working with them. Determination comes first; the boy definitely has to want to run and be willing to sacrifice for the cause of running. It does not take too long to discover this quality—just a few hard workouts.

The second quality is endurance—and this depends on the physiological makeup of the body. During the cross-country season, I determine if a boy can build endurance to the point where he will be able to develop as a distance runner.

NOTE: I feel that if I have someone who has these two qualities, I will not be wasting my time or theirs. How good a runner a boy becomes will not depend entirely on determination and endurance; speed, running style, and psychological makeup all play a part.

METHODS AND APPROACHES

There are a number of methods and approaches in training distance runners. Many coaches, I am sure, combine certain of the following techniques and some go strictly by one method. Here, I will cover briefly some of the more popular ways of developing and conditioning distance runners.

Fartlek Training: The simplest definition for this type of training is *a combination of alternate hard running with recovery running on a track or challenging terrain.* An example would be to sprint hard for 100 yards, slow down to an easy pace for a short distance to recuperate, and then resume hard running again.

In order to get maximum effect, this should be incorporated into a 3- or 4-mile total distance, depending upon the ability of your runners. I use this method of training intermittently on the track. We sprint hard for 200 yards, slow down to curves. The weakness of this system is that if you do not have dedicated athletes, they often will spend too much time recuperating between sprints.

Interval Training: This is a system of repeated efforts, using a specific distance and a short recovery period after each effort. In my cross-country program, I use 440 intervals at 70-75 seconds with a 440 jog for recovery. When this program is first started, one must be careful not to overload the runner. I feel it is best to build up to your interval program with over-distance training. After approximately two weeks of over-distance running during the cross-country season, I start my interval program.

NOTE: The first week of interval training we use 6 x 440, and work up to 20 x 440 intervals the week just prior to the state meet. When a boy can carry a work load of 20 x 440's at 75 seconds and hold at this pace with a 440 jog between, he is getting close to good running form.

Oregon System: This system was introduced by Bill Bowerman, track coach at the University of Oregon. This program consists of a variety of work-outs—interval training with a gradual increase in speed so that a runner is not "hung" on a certain pace. Fartlek training is also used and is a very important phase of this system. Also emphasized are strenuous workouts one day, followed by a much less strenuous work-out the next. This tends to build the athlete faster than continuous hard work day after day, with no time for recuperation.

NOTE: I have briefly described just three types of training programs; there are, of course, many more. I try to incorporate some of each of the previously mentioned programs into my schedule, along with some of my own ideas. It is very important, I believe, for the coach to understand and use al¹ positive factors that will help a person become a better runner—and at the same time, eliminate the negative factors that tend to distract the runner.

TRAINING SCHEDULE

I will briefly outline the training schedule for our cross-country runners (Chart 1) that we try to follow at Shelby High School. I feel that this portion of the total program is as important as the training period during our regular track season.

NOTE: It is at this time that I can build endurance as well as evaluate the potential of each runner. You will notice that during this phase we use over-distance, fartlek, and interval training.

Our cross-country season starts in August and ends in October. Notice that the first week we hold a training camp (at Flathead Lake). During this week, we run 6 to 8 miles twice a day. This has proven to be very profitable, not only in terms of conditioning but also in building interest in the program. We camp outside and really enjoy ourselves with swimming, hiking, fishing, along with running.

OTHER METHODS

In addition to our work schedule, we have our gym open at 7 a.m. each weekday morning for light workouts. This is not a requirement, but most of the better runners are dedicated and take advantage of the facility.

During the months of November, December, January, and February, the boys work out on their own. However, many of the track people are involved in basketball or wrestling—and this not only keeps them in shape, but also gives them a break from the routine of just running.

During the regular track season, our training schedule is much the same as the cross-country schedule, with the exception of the interval portion. I feel that if we use strictly 440's, it becomes drudgery for the runners and also makes it easy to get hung up on one pace. I mix repeat 220's, 330's, 550's, 660's, and 880's in the interval program to build speed and conditioning and to quicken the pace.

Chart 1

Training Schedule

MONTH	WEEK	DAY	TYPE OF TRAINING	DISTANCE
Aug.	3rd	Mon.-Sat.	Training Camp	6-8 miles, twice per day
,,	4th	Mon.-Sat.	Over-distance	6-8 miles per day
Sept.	1st	M,W,F	Over-distance	6-8 miles per day
		Tues., Thurs.	Interval	6 x 440's, 70-75 sec.
,,	2nd	M,W,F	Over-distance	6-8 miles
		Tues., Thurs.	Interval	8 x 440's, 70-75 sec.
,,	3rd	M,W,F	Fartlek	3 miles
		Tues., Thurs.	Interval	10 x 440's, 70-75 sec.
,,	4th	M,W	Interval	14 x 440's, 70-75 sec.
		Tues., Thurs.	Over-distance	6-8 miles
		Fri.	Speed work	20 x 100's on grass
		Sat.	Meet	
Oct.	1st	M,W	Interval	16 x 440's, 70-75 sec.
		Tues., Thurs.	Fartlek	4 miles
		Fri.	Speed work	10 x 100's on grass
		Sat.	Meet	
,,	2nd	M,W	Interval	18 x 440's, 70-75 sec.
		Tues.	2 miles for time	
		Thurs.	Fartlek	4 miles
		Fri.	Speed work	10 x 100's on grass
		Sat.	Meet	
,,	3rd	M,W	Interval	20 x 440's, 70-75 sec.
		Tues., Thurs.	Fartlek	4 miles
		Fri.	Speed work	10 x 100's on grass
		Sat.	Meet	
,,	4th	Mon.	Over-distance	4 miles
		Tues.	Light fartlek	6 miles
		Wed.	Over-distance	2 miles
		Thurs.	Over-distance	3 miles
		Fri.	Leave for state meet	Light jogging to loosen up
		Sat.	State meet	

Part VI

Shot, Discus, Javelin

1

Achieving Shot Put Form

by Aubrey Bonham

Former Head Track Coach
Whittier (California) College

*Aubrey Bonham coached at Whittier College for over
30 years before retiring in 1968. He coached many individual champions and won the college section of the Drake
Relays three different years in the mile, 880 and 440 relays.*

All coaches know that *form* in the weight events is just as important, if not more so, than strength. Anyone can know the correct thing
to do, but the difficult thing is to know how to achieve it. During my
coaching experience, I have found the following five factors to be of
utmost importance to the success of the shot putter. My suggestions on
how to achieve correct form and avoid faults follow each factor.

1. Balance in the Put: The back ring dip should be a controlled,
rhythmical speed pick up with the left foot pull and the drive-shove off

the right foot perfectly synchronized. All action to the center of the ring must be kept in a straight line so that the putter can achieve maximum body thrust and ring speed.

SUGGESTION: The coach should put a mark on the toe board for the putter's left foot and one in the center of the ring for his right. The putter should then practice hitting these marks with and without the shot. To keep the putter's head at the proper attitude, thus greatly aiding balance, the coach can place a marker for eye fixation 20 to 25 feet in back of the ring.

2. Height in Lifting and Thrusting: The number-one essential in shot putting is that the athlete keep his weight over a bent right leg until he starts the actual throw. He must keep the shot back. If he doesn't, the "rifle shot" put straight from the shoulder results. Remember, once the shot is started forward from the right foot, it is very difficult to add height to the throw.

SUGGESTION: The putter should practice coming across the ring low and flat, saying "lift" just before the right foot strikes position. To enable the putter to achieve proper height, the coach can place three colored wires 20 to 30 feet from the ring at different heights (according to the athlete's strength). These can serve as lift and push targets.

3. Center Ring Hesitation: This is a fault that cuts down distance. It is caused by the putter's failing to get maximum shoulder cock *at the beginning of the put*. He tries to compensate by getting it in the middle of the put and breaks the straight line motion to the center of the ring. This is bad; very bad.

SUGGESTION: The putter should practice exaggerating the shoulder cock when he takes his initial stance. He should maintain this shoulder position until the right foot reaches position and then explode with the right side.

4. Arm Action and Follow-Through: The arm action must be "grooved" so that the arm explodes the final lift and pushes the shot out. The arm and fingers must stay with the ball until the last possible second.

5. *The Reverse:* The reverse must come late, *but fast!* If it comes too soon, the athlete will throw with both feet in the air. You can not push on air. If it comes too late, he will foul.

> SUGGESTION: The athlete should practice half reverses and then late full reverses. The second the shot leaves the fingertips, the reverse is executed.

A 12-Pound Shot in a Size 16

by David Star

Director of Athletics
New Hyde Park (New York) High School

David Star is director of athletics at New Hyde Park (New Hyde Park, New York) High School, where his track squads have seen their share of winning seasons. The following is a fine example of creative coaching.

One of our weight men threw the indoor 12-pound shot 49 to 50 feet quite consistently as a junior, and I predicted great things for him.

When the nice weather arrived I looked forward with anticipation to his first efforts with the smaller 12-pound metal shot, but I was disagreeably surprised. He was unable to toss the regular 12-pounder as far as the larger indoor 12-pound shot. In fact, he was way off—by three to four feet.

He claimed he couldn't handle the smaller shot; he didn't feel comfortable with it. I wondered whether this was a psychological quirk, but decided to give him the benefit of the doubt and secure a larger 12-pound shot if possible.

Technological Problems: Sporting goods people told me it would be technologically difficult to get by with only 12 pounds of metal in a 16-pound mold. They also felt that using a hollow center sphere about the size of a golf ball would not succeed because it would crack when surrounded by molten metal.

Two manufacturers stated that the project would be prohibitive either because of expense or because of design. Then I wondered whether the 16-pound shot might not be reduced by four pounds without sacrificing size. That would solve my boy's problem.

A machinist agreed to try to drill four pounds out of the 16-pound shot. He drilled holes a shade under one-half inch, and when I returned to pick up the shot it looked like a swiss cheese because it took about 60 holes to bring the weight down to the desired level.

That was not 12 pounds but 11½, because the machinist and I figured it would take about one-half pound of wood to fill the holes and round out the original shape.

Three-foot dowel sticks one-half inch in diameter were purchased, cut into two-inch lengths, and tapped into the holes. They fit snugly and the ends were sanded to conform with the contour of the ball.

Mission Accomplished: I now had an oversized 12-pound shot, and all that was left to do was find out whether the experiment had been worthwhile or merely a waste of money.

Our junior hadn't thrown the shot in more than a month, but on his first try with the improvised shot he bettered 48 feet with ease. I conceded that he had been right all along, that his trouble was physical, not mental.

Most boys throw the outdoor shot farther than the indoor, but our junior was the oddity. I figured the larger size permitted him more wrist action.

During his senior year the boy's progress was normal, with outdoor tosses with the large shot better than indoor throws. The time, thought, and effort spent had been useful.

3

Strength Training for the Shot and Discus

by J.L. Mayhew

Physical Education Instructor
University of Illinois

by Bill Riner

Head Track Coach
Buford (Lancaster, South Carolina) High School

Before joining the department of physical education at the University of Illinois (Champaign, Illinois), Jerry Mayhew was assistant cross-country and track coach at Appalachian State (Boone, North Carolina) University. The cross-country mark was 27-8 for that period. Bill Riner is head track coach at Buford (Lancaster, South Carolina) High School. He was conference Coach-of-the-Year in 1971 and his team won the championship.

It goes almost without saying that it takes strength and power to perform in the weight events of track and field. Certainly agility, coordination, and balance are important, but several studies have indicated that these factors can also be improved in conjunction with strength through weight training.

NOTE: Research has shown progressive resistance exercise (PRE) to be the most beneficial method for developing strength and power. It is an accepted fact that an athlete can develop more size (hypertrophy) and strength through weight-training exercises than through repetitive gravity resistant exercises. Isometrics do not offer the motivation of moving a weighted bar, and indications are that the strength gained is specific to the exercise position.

Most coaches are aware that a man with strength and skill is a better performer than one with skill alone. Therefore, the complete shot and/or discus program should include a comprehensive weight-training routine prior to and during every season. Increased strength aids in ease of handling the implement, velocity of delivery, and prevention of injury, and generally improves the performance potential of the athlete. These factors have long been recognized by the great weight men and form a primary basis of their success.

PRINCIPLES OF THE PROGRAM

The following suggestions are designed to allow the coach to employ a sound, scientific program of progressive resistance within the total track program. There are many PRE devices which offer shortcuts to strength gains. The primary point of concern to the coach is that strength built in a short period is lost rapidly.

The program to be employed is a weight-training routine using progressively increasing loads to develop maximum strength. The basic principles include the following:

● The weight should be moved through the full range of joint movement. This prevents the athlete from becoming muscle-bound and provides a dynamic strength.

● The weight employed for each exercise differs for each athlete and must be arrived at individually through trial and error. A specified percentage of the body weight for any exercise will not serve all athletes and may even hinder more than it will help. Each load must be determined by the individual for his specific strength ability.

● The most widely accepted method of repetitions for strength gains lies between six and 10 per set. Three sets for each exercise is the usual dosage—although, for some purposes, as many as six sets may be employed. There is no definite number of sets or repetitions that must be used.

● The program should include exercises for the entire body, but primarily the big-muscle groups. It does very little good in the throwing events to have great strength in the arms if the legs are weak.

● One should always lift with a partner if possible. In employing heavily loaded barbells, the possibility of accidents is always present. The best insurance against this is to have one or more "spotters" assisting for each exercise.

● A good warm-up should precede any work with the weights. This may range from jogging to working with light barbells to ready the muscles for the task ahead.

● The big-muscle exercises that require a great deal of energy and employ heavy weights should be done early in the routine while the athlete is still fresh, alert, and guarding against mishaps. However, be certain such lifting is preceded by a good warm-up to avoid injury.

CORE EXERCISES

The exercise routine to be employed by various individuals may vary widely. However, it is important to include the bulk-building, big-muscle exercises for all throwers and to allow specialists to employ unique or specific exercises at the conclusion of the routine. Making up the basic core of the exercise routine are exercises which work the shoulder girdle, torso, back, and legs.

NOTE: The following exercises are recommended as the basic core of the thrower's routine:

1. Bench Press: The spotter should assist in positioning the bar above the chest while the lifter is in the supine position. The bar should be lowered to the midsternal position; it should not be bounced off the chest because of potential danger to the ribs and sternum. Such "cheating" does not aid the athlete, even with the potentially greater weight that he can handle. If the hand grip position on the bar is narrow, the major benefit is received by the triceps. If the grip is wide, the major work is done by the pectoral muscles.

2. Half Squat: The half squat develops the quadriceps muscles; in addition, the last 15 degrees of extension is accomplished by the hamstring muscles. The spotter should assist the lifter in positioning the weight across the trapezius muscle to prevent damage to the vertebrae. A towel or foam rubber pad may be wrapped around the bar to further protect the neck. If no power rack is available, a bench or chair should be placed under the lifter to maintain the half squat position.

3. Seated Press: This exercise isolates the shoulder musculature and triceps. It also prevents damage to the lower back which often results from a standing Olympic type press. The spotter should assist the lifter in positioning the bar at shoulder level while the lifter is in the seated position. The lifter should split his legs front-to-back in the seated position in order to maintain his balance with the heavily loaded bar.

4. Straight-Legged Deadlift: The lower back and gluteal muscles, providing a strong base for action, should be exercised heavily. Care should be taken when performing this movement not to strain the lower back. The force applied to the bar should be slowly administered and not jerky. The grip should be an alternate one: one hand facing forward and one facing backward for more stability.

5. Weighted Sit-Ups: The abdominal muscles form the front of the torso and give strength to the base. The sit-up should be done with the feet anchored and the knees bent (to isolate action on the abdominal muscles). A weight plate may be held behind the head. It can be made progressive by additional weight behind the head or by using an incline board.

6. Toe Raises: A strong calf muscle contributes to the integrity of the knee joint as well as strengthening the initial drive phase in the shot. The spotter should assist in positioning the bar as in the half squat. The toes should be placed on a 2-inch board to increase the range of movement. (This exercise should be done in a power rack if possible.)

7. Biceps Curl: The bar should be gripped at shoulder width and the movement performed (1) with no back bend or (2) with the aid of a backward lean. The former isolates development on the biceps while the latter allows the back muscles to contribute to the movement. The "cheat" (backward lean) curl usually can be accomplished with more weight.

NOTE: The above exercises form a basic core and do not include special exercises that concentrate on isolated parts of the body.

LIFTING PROBLEMS

Two psychological factors must be considered when employing a weight program:

● In the early stages of the program (first two to three weeks), some individuals may make what appears to be great gains in strength. Actually, a complex movement that requires a great deal of coordination will have a learning factor; as the individual learns to handle the weight in a particular lift he is able to use more weight.

NOTE: Do not confuse this early learning with actual strength gains.

● The other factor is the problem of "leveling off" or "going stale." Gains in strength are not gradual or linear. Instead, they follow a staircase design, with plateaus punctuating the gaining phases. When such plateaus are reached, the athlete should change his routine slightly or lay off for a few days.

YEARLY PATTERN

The yearly pattern of weight training often followed is to lift three days per week and avoid all throwing during the off-season, and reverse the process during the season.

This routine is incorrect in that off-season work should include throwing practice. This maintains the neuromuscular pattern of throwing while the new strength is being built.

During the competitive season, the frequency of lifting may be reduced, but it should be continued in order to maintain the new level of strength.

CONCLUSION

The stronger thrower is potentially the better thrower. His ability to achieve his maximum potential is greater, as is his resistance to injury. The increased bulk built through weight training provides for greater dynamic power in imparting velocity to the implement thrown. The complete shot-discus program should include a well-balanced weight-training program.

4

Discus-Throwing Technique

By Ralph B. Maughan

Head Track Coach
Utah State (Logan, Utah) University

Ralph Maughan has been coaching high school and college track since 1948, and has been head track coach at Utah State since 1951. During that time he has coached such greats as L. Jay Silvester, a one-time holder of the world record (199'-2½") in the discus; N.C.A.A. discus champion (Glenn Passey); three Pan-American game winners; two Olympians and eight track All-Americans. Coach Maughan is a frequent lecturer at track clinics.

In my opinion, balance, throwing position acceleration and release are by far the most important parts of a discus throw. Sheer strength, although it helps, is relatively unimportant. For example, Jay Silvester was a 230 pound powerhouse when he made his throw of 199' 2½". Glenn Passey weighs 174 pounds and, compared to Silves-

Figure 1

ter, is slight; yet his unofficial throw (using the same form as Jay) of 196′ proves that form is all-important in the discus. Here is the form we use for the discus at Utah State—it is *championship* form.

Initial Stance and Preliminary Swings: The thrower must begin with his back to the direction of the throw. Some throwers are coached to swing the left foot into position after standing sideways to the direction of the throw. I believe that this causes too hurried a start and an improper placing of the left foot at the back of the ring. The thrower's feet are spread shoulder width. The right foot is against the back of the ring and the left about 2 or 3 inches from the ring. Weight should be equally distributed. Preliminary swings should be easy and few in number. They serve three purposes: (1) to loosen up waist and shoulders; (2) to relax the thrower; and (3) to prepare him mentally for the throw.

> THE PERFECT THROW: Tell your thrower that, *at all times* during his preliminary swings, he should try to think of what the perfect throw feels like. This will put him in the right frame of mind for a good throw.

The Body Turn: When the thrower feels that he is ready to spin, he should bring the discus as far back as he can, without losing balance. This will bring the left heel high off the circle surface, and the weight over the flexed right knee and leg (Figure 1). The body should be erect, but twisted at the waist. He then begins his spin by first assuming a slight sitting position and then transferring his weight from the right foot to the ball of the left foot (Figure 2).

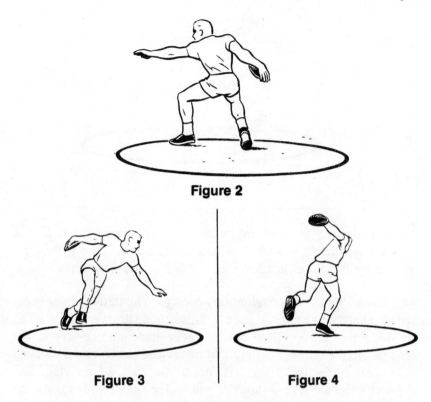

Figure 2

Figure 3   **Figure 4**

NOTE: It is important that *all* the weight is transferred to the left foot and that the left heel does not touch the circle. All the driving is done from the ball and toes of the right foot. Remember, the body is turned with the legs, *not* the discus.

The thrower then swings his slightly flexed right leg around in a wide sweeping motion, being sure to keep his right knee and foot out and away from the left leg (Figure 3). He actually leads with the right foot, rather than the knee as in the run-over type of turn. As soon as the right foot has swung to about the 10 o'clock position, the thrower throws it down and inward forcefully to the center of the ring and snaps off from the ball of the left foot (Figures 3 and 4).

DOWN AND IN: If the right foot is thrown out across the circle, the thrower will jump around rather than turning with a smooth skip or snap. Throwing the right foot down and *in* eliminates this jumping action which hampers the acceleration of the first turn.

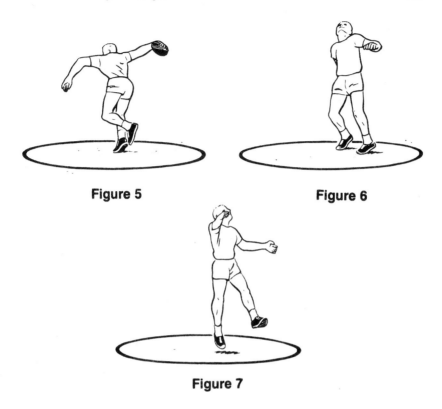

Figure 5   **Figure 6**

Figure 7

This will snap him around and propel him across the ring. The left foot is picked up sharply and is brought past, and relatively close, to the right leg. It is snapped down 2 or 3 feet from the right foot (Figure 5).

TWO TURNS: The thrower should think of the spin and throw as two turns—the second being much faster than the first. You want continued acceleration from where the right foot is thrown down and in to where the discus is released.

The Throwing Position: The thrower has now completed his turn and lands in the throwing position. Just as the left foot touches the surface of the circle, the thrower must start the throw with a terrific surge of power in the right leg. The left leg also lifts with all available power. This comes a fraction of a second after the right.

What you have practically is a double leg drive, with the thrower generating as much power as he can (Figure 6). The discus should be held as far back as possible until the right leg begins its drive. At this time, the discus must be lifted from behind the hip with as much speed as the thrower can muster. This will cause him to reverse properly. The discus is released after the feet leave the ground (Figure 7).

The shoulders should at all times be square and parallel to the ground. The head and eyes must be kept on a level plane. There should be no ducking or raising of the head and eyes. If the thrower keeps his head down, it will pull his chest in. He *must* have his head *up* and his chest *out* to be able to throw properly. The left arm should be slightly bent and should be carried away from the body with the left wrist on the same plane as the right hand carrying the discus. The proper action of the left arm during the throw should be a terrific whipping motion of the slightly bent arm led by the left wrist up and across the chest and then forcefully down and back. Think of throwing the discus with the shoulders—this gives proper left arm action. As the discus is released, the right hand must be shut forcefully to insure proper grip and thumb pressure on the discus.

5

Javelin-Throwing Technique

by Douglas Raubenheimer

Head Track Coach
Hanover Park (New Jersey) High School

Douglas Raubenheimer has been teaching and coaching at Hanover Park (New Jersey) High School for the past 14 years. During that time, he has compiled a dual meet record of 89-35, which includes 5 conference championships.

I believe that throwing the javelin is one of the most difficult of all field events. It requires (as do all field events) agility, strength and coordination. But more than that, it requires *perfection* in the technical area. Technique in throwing consists of the following five points or steps. The thrower must perfect *all* of them to be successful. Here is how we coach them at Hanover Park:

Figure 1

The Grip: I coach all my javelin men to use what we call the "V" grip (Figure 1). This grip consists of holding the javelin immediately behind the whip cord between the second and third fingers with the thumb and other fingers placed along the whip cord. This grip is probably the most difficult to learn, but once mastered, the distance achieved through its use will exceed that of any other grip. There will be a tendency for the tip of the javelin to float to the side instead of pointing straight ahead. There will also be a tendency to twist the wrist. Time and concentration will overcome these faults.

The Approach: I think that taking a long, fast run prior to the release of the javelin is not necessary. We have found that when one of our men tries to sprint, it becomes necessary for him to "chop" his steps in order to achieve the proper footwork in the release sector. Striding for a distance of approximately 20 yards has proven to be successful with our javelin throwers. In this approach, the javelin should be held high with the elbow at shoulder level. The throwing arm should not be held rigid, but should be kept moving back and forth *slightly* with each stride. The tip of the javelin should be pointed straight ahead or slightly upward.

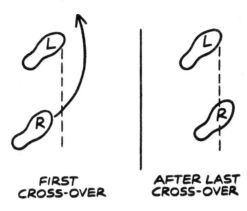

FIRST CROSS-OVER

AFTER LAST CROSS-OVER

Figure 2

Footwork: Rather than coaching a series of complicated steps, I teach the boys only two cross-over steps. They have been most successful using this less complicated method. As the steps are begun, the left side of the body is turned in the direction of the throw. The left foot is placed at a 45° angle (to direction of the throw) and is slightly to the right of center (Figure 2). At the same time, the right arm is dropped, fully extended, behind the body. The javelin shaft is held along the side of the arm and the tip points up at an angle of approximately 30° (Figure 3).

FULL EXTENSION: It is of the utmost importance that the throwing arm be fully extended in order for the thrower to achieve maximum throwing power.

The first cross-over step is made by crossing the right foot over the left, lifting the left and placing it down ahead of the right in the manner previously mentioned. (The cross-over steps are more like "skips" than they are like steps.) The second cross-over is made in much the same way as the first with the exception that the left foot is now placed slightly to the left side, thus opening the body for the throw.

The Release: To execute the release, the thrower should rotate the trunk of his body to the left. At the same time, he brings his throwing arm forward in a motion similar to that of a catcher throwing a baseball. It is important that the elbow lead the throw, the hand of the

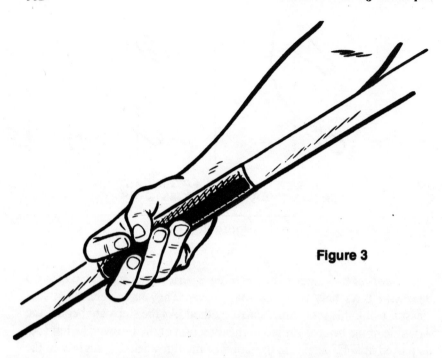

Figure 3

throwing arm pass close to the ear, and the point of the javelin be held straight and not allowed to drift out to the right. The javelin should leave the thrower's hand at an angle of 45° and the wrist should be snapped forward (not twisted) to apply maximum strength to the javelin.

The Follow-Through: The follow-through with the right arm should be straight down, not across the body. This prevents the tail of the javelin from being pulled down. To guard against fouling, it is important that the thrower hop onto his right foot behind the throwing line. He *should not* watch the flight of the javelin, but rather his right foot to prevent it from landing on or over the line.

6

Common Faults in Throwing the Javelin

by Ronald J. Hayes

Chairman of the Health and Physical Education Department
Middlesex (New Jersey) High School

> *During his years as track coach, Ronald Hayes com-*
> *piled a record of 28-7; he was in charge of the weight men.*
> *He is presently line coach for the football squad and Chair-*
> *man of the Health and Physical Education Department.*

I began coaching the weight men some years ago with no previous track experience other than my physical education training. While one of the boys I worked with was Central Jersey Group II champ—and improved his distance over 30 feet—this boy and others did not reach expected potential.

NOTE: I analyzed the season, researched the subject, and came up with a checklist of common faults in throwing the javelin. These should be beneficial to beginning coaches who are faced with a similar situation.

The Grip: There are three acceptable grips for holding the javelin. These are the American, the Finnish, and the Hungarian styles. The American grip has the index finger and the thumb on the tuck of the cord, with the javelin resting in the palm of the hand. The Finnish grip consists of the second finger and thumb on the tuck of the cord, and the first finger lies curled slightly behind the second. The Hungarian grip consists of the index finger extended along the shaft of the javelin. According to Bankhead and Thorsen, any of these three grips are acceptable to use, and the thrower must choose the one that is the most comfortable for him.

Common Faults to Look For in Gripping the Javelin:

1. *Gripping too tightly*: Grip tight enough to control.
2. *Javelin not in the palm of hand*: The javelin should lie in the palm of the hand.

Selection of Javelin: Select a javelin that will give you the largest possible lifting surface area, the highest possible stiffness, and a tilting movement that allows the javelin to make a mark in the ground. Javelins are designed with different diameters up to a maximum diameter of 35 millimeters. The larger the diameter of the javelin, the greater the throwing distance. This does not mean that every javelin thrower should choose a javelin with the thickest diameter. Choose a javelin that is comfortable when you are learning to throw. When you have reached your desired distance, switch to a javelin that has a thicker diameter. It is time to change to a thicker javelin when you have reached your greatest possible distance and your javelin lands with a steep angle. For maximum distance, you are looking for the smallest possible angle that permits the javelin to make a mark in the ground.

Common Faults Made in Selecting a Javelin:

1. *Selecting a javelin that is too thick* : Choose a javelin that fits comfortably in the hand. When you feel you have reached your farthest possible distance, change to a thicker javelin.
2. *Selecting a javelin that vibrates*: Choose a javelin that vibrates as little as possible. If there is too much vibration, the javelin is too thin.

The Approach: Four different approaches are commonly used for getting into position to throw the javelin. There are two American and two Finnish approaches. One American approach is the hop-step style where the thrower hops after hitting the check mark, then steps into the position for throwing. The second American style is the rear cross-step, where the right leg is placed behind the left in a cross-step, prior to the throwing position. The first Finnish style is the front cross-step, where the right leg crosses in front of the left in a cross-step prior to the throwing position. The second Finnish is a combination hop and front cross-step prior to throwing. An analysis of experts states that the world's best throwers use the Finnish crossover style. This particular style allows for a faster and longer run and the thrower is not required to run at full speed during the approach.

The Carry: There are three acceptable methods of carriage. They also are Finnish and American. One American carry consists of carrying the javelin over the shoulder with the point slightly higher than horizontal. The second American carry has the arm down, extended backward, with the tip of the javelin held high. The palm of the hand points away from the body so that the wrist does not rotate. It appears that most coaches recommend the Finnish style as the best method. This consists of carrying the javelin above the right shoulder with the point down.

Common Faults Made in the Approach and Carry:

1. *Starting too fast:* Half speed for about the first five or six steps, never at full speed.

2. *Missing checks marks and failing to increase speed proportionately:* Practice steps over and over, starting at slow speeds and increasing speed when you are able to hit your check marks. Measure the check marks so they are always accurate. Be sure speed is increased at check marks and be sure speed is controlled.

3. *Uncontrolled run:* Be sure you coordinate the movement of the javelin with the run.

4. *Failure to keep javelin facing straight forward during approach:* Keeping your eyes on the point of the javelin will keep it straight.

5. *Inconsistent count pattern of number of steps:* You must count

steps as they are taken so you hit check marks accurately; after you become skilled this should be automatic.

6. *Failure to keep your body and feet straight to the front*: Keeping eyes on the point of javelin will help keep the body straight.

7. *Failure to execute the proper steps correctly*: You must be able to execute the proper steps, which can be learned by slow-motion drills on the step selection you choose. After the steps are learned, they can be combined with the run and throw.

8. *Stopping before throwing*: You have to transfer speed into throwing force for a long-distance throw. This cannot be done if the thrower stops before throwing. Practice combining run into steps to throw.

9. *Failure to execute a semi-reverse after throw to avoid fouling*: Bring the right foot around so it is parallel to scratch line, this will semi-reverse the body.

Delivery, Release, and Recovery: A delivery, release, and recovery should be used that allows the thrower to get his body into the best possible position for a comfortable throw. This will depend a great deal on the type of approach used to place the body in the proper throwing position.

Common Faults Made in the Delivery, Release, and Recovery:

1. *Pausing when transferring run into delivery*: There must be a continuous movement from run to delivery, with no great loss of speed when transferring force into delivery.

2. *Javelin out of alignment when bringing arm back*: Keep eye on point of javelin.

3. *Incomplete arm drawback*: The arm should be extended back so that the tip almost touches the ground. This should be easier when the body is turned properly to the right.

4. *Delivery from the side rather than over the shoulder*: Leading over the right shoulder with the elbow will help keep the proper delivery.

5. *Imbalance during delivery*: Too short a step or too much of a lean backward prior to the throw causes imbalance.

6. *Releasing at an angle too high or low*: The proper angle for release is 45°. A longer and greater pull of the arm and proper shift of weight off the right foot to the left, will help give the proper release angle.

7. *Release before full force applied to javelin*: The same explanation as number six.

8. *Taking too short a stride when getting set for delivery*: A long stride puts the body into proper position for the throw; a stride that is short will result in number six and seven.

Conclusion: To develop a good javelin thrower, pick out the style that is best suited for giving maximum distance and comfort to him. Then develop the thrower to his maximum potential by avoiding the faults described in this article.

7

Specialized Isometric Training for the Javelin Throw

by Raymond Frey

Head Track Coach
St. Johnsbury (Vermont) Academy

> *Raymond Frey has been head track coach at St. Johnsbury (Vermont) Academy for the past 17 years. During that time, he has compiled a meet record of 94-23-2. His squads have captured 9 league championships, 7 district championships and 8 state championships, and have enjoyed 8 undefeated seasons.*

During the last decade, weight training and athletics have become synonymous. Since nearly all weight training improves performance, a speicalized training can improve it still more.

NOTE: Over the past few seasons, I have employed a simple exercise designed to simulate the throwing technique for our javelin men. The activity has paid off big dividends through the years.

We use four basic positions, but the athlete can adopt more if he chooses. The equipment required is simply a strong rope approximately 3 feet long with a knot tied at one end. The other end is secured to one of our isometric contraction racks. The four basic positions follow.

Photo 1: The thrower grips the rope at the knotted end, using his normal javelin grip, and assumes his initial throwing position—the position arrived at after the run-up and cross-over step. His rear foot is planted and his lead foot is extended to offer balance.

EXECUTION: Exerting isometric force, he applies pressure to his major and minor pectoral muscles, as well as to his intercostal right side rib cage.

Photo 2: In Photo 2 the thrower is beginning the whip action with both feet firmly planted on the floor.

EXECUTION: By this exercise he is strengthening his trapezius muscle.

Photo 3: In Photo 3 the thrower's arm is over his right ear, and his hand is placed over his elbow. This is one of the most critical throwing positions.

EXECUTION: This exercise provides an excellent teaching device whereby the coach can instruct the correct form. The main muscle of the shoulder, the deltoid, is developed in this position.

Photo 4: In Photo 4 the arm is almost fully extended—just before the release. The accent of stress is placed on the triceps.

EXECUTION: Again, aside from the strengthening exercise, the thrower's form can be corrected in this position and he can be brought to concentrate on the proper release angle.

Repetitions: Our boys begin with three seconds in each position—building up over the weeks to three repetitions at eight seconds. This series of exercises is simply incorporated into the regular weight-training workout.

Photo 1

Photo 2

Photo 3

Photo 4

NOTE: Shot put and discus competitors can also benefit from this type of drill—by simply setting up a second rope with a loop tied at one end. The insertion of the hand in the loop enables the shot put and discus men to assume their natural throwing positions while utilizing isometric contraction training. TIP: Have the men wear a glove to prevent a possible rope burn.

Part VII

Pole Vault, High Jump

1

Developing the High School Pole Vaulter

by Don Harshbarger

Physical Education Instructor
Naperville (Illinois) Public Schools

Don Harshbarger is Physical Education instructor for the Naperville Public Schools (Illinois), and a former track coach from Oak Park (Illinois) High School, where pole vaulting was his specialty. In the 20 years that he has been coaching track, his teams have won various championships and three of his pole vaulters were state champs.

Without doubt, pole vaulting is the most complicated of track events. The prospect must be an acrobat, a tumbler, a fast runner, a strong lad and a patient one. Plus that, it takes a lot of just plain "guts." How many boys would even jump from a height of 14 or more feet, let alone being upside down at this height and trying to come down feet first!

Starting from scratch, then, here's how I recommend developing the high school pole vaulter:

ABOUT THE POLE: I believe that beginners should be taught the principles of vaulting on a steel pole. The point is contradicted. Some think that using the fiber pole at the start is an advantage because less vaulting form is required; the fiber-glass pole vaulter depends on the whip of the pole to get the extra height. But I say start the beginner right.

The Run: Most high school boys run too far. I recommend a run of no more than 100 feet; 80 to 90 feet is preferred. The vaulter should stand with his feet together on the starting mark. Make a line about 1 foot ahead of this starting mark. The boy should always step on this line with the same foot to assure him of the same start. About half way to the box make another check mark. The vaulter should hit this second mark while running at his vaulting speed.

COACHING TIP: Have him practice this much of the run until he can constantly hit this second check mark.

Now have the vaulter put the pole in the box. Extend his arms over his head while he holds the pole. A line straight down from his hands will be about right for a temporary take mark. Have him start from his first mark (the starting mark) and hit the second mark, then continue on to the take mark. This work should not be done on the runway but off to one side.

COACHING TIP: The vaulter must not watch for this take mark, but the coach must watch to see where the take-off foot is hitting. If after three trials the marks vary, take the middle one and have the vaulter repeat until he is hitting close to the same spot all the time.

Carrying the Pole: It doesn't make too much difference at what height the upper or right hand grips the pole—but let's start at 9 feet. The palm is up. The distance between the hands will also vary; the weight of the pole (most are very light now) determines the distance. Sixteen inches apart is a good distance. The left hand grips the pole with the palm down. The thumbs of the hands are pointing toward the small end of the pole. The forearm of the left arm should be parallel to the chest, with the right hand gripping the pole (not too tight) just behind the hip. Next, have the vaulter lift the point of the pole just above the horizontal position. Make certain that the pole does not wobble from side to side but is always pointed directly toward or above the vaulting box.

COACHING TIP: Have the boy practice hitting his check marks. If he misses the first mark, he should stop and start over. It is necessary that he hit this mark every time. The coach or another vaulter can check his take-off mark. He must never look at this mark because his eyes should be on the vaulting box.

Vaulting Form: The secret of vaulting is to keep the pole close to some part of the body, keeping one half of the body on one side of the pole. Here are the distinct movements involved in proper vaulting form:

1. *The take off.* The left foot must hit the mark directly under the extended arms, just *after* the pole has hit the end of the box. It *must not* come down first. As this take-off foot hits the mark, the pole is raised over the head. The right knee should be raised as the vaulter takes off. His head and left elbow should be on the left side of the pole, and the pole diagonal across the body. As he takes off, he must catch up with the pole, knees high, and double up so that one half of the body will be behind the pole and one half ahead. He rides in this position until all forward and upward momentum is lost.

2. *The pull up.* The body must straighten. The legs shoot up—the right cutting across the left, which turns the vaulter over. He pulls with the right arm and pushes with the left. The pole must be close to the right shoulder during this movement. Once this pull up and turn over is accomplished, the vaulter is ready to release. He lets go of the pole with the left hand, turning the thumb in, which will enable the left elbow to clear the bar. He should swing the left arm out and over the head and push hard with the right.

3. *The cut down.* As the left arm is swung over the head, the left leg cuts down over the bar. As the left leg cuts down, it lifts the head and shoulders. The vaulter now releases the right hand and throws this arm high into the air, turning the thumb in as he releases. He should come down, feet first.

NOTE: No two vaulters will vault exactly the same. The timing of the movements—swing ride, pull up, turn over and release—will vary. Some will be "fly away" vaulters; they just get up there and let go, letting their momentum throw them through the air. But most of these vaulters aren't consistent.

Practice: It would be foolhardy to tell a lad to use his steps and vault; it isn't that easy. I have seen only two boys who could pick up a pole, take a short run and vault 10 feet. I like to tell the boy to get back about 30 feet from the box, run and stick the pole, and just ride the pole all the way into the pit. This teaches him to become a part of the pole. See that he gets one-half of his body on each side of the pole. Have him double up, knees near the chest. He should lift his right knee on the take off and look at the back of the box. He can pull into this doubled position but do not let him turn over. He can practice this 50 times a night, using the short run.

COACHING TIP: After you feel that he knows what the pole is for, have him take this short run and add the turn over to his vault. Continue this until he can ride the pole, turn over and land on his feet in the pit. Once he has accomplished the correct vaulting form (and not until then), can you put him on the full run.

Training Tips: Here are the training tips I recommend:

1. Use the weights during the off season and three nights a week while training.
2. Climb the rope every day.
3. Use grip developers.
4. Sprint, getting the knees exceptionally high.
5. Do leg lifts and sit-ups to develop the abdominal muscles.
6. Do push-ups and walk on hands.
7. Jump from a height of 12 to 14 feet into a pit. It will teach you to relax as you fall.

2

Coaching the Pole Vault

by Henry Thomson

Head Track Coach
Shoreline (Seattle, Washington) Community College

> *Henry Thomson became head track coach at Shoreline Community College in 1965 after a successful high school coaching career at Shoreline High School. Under Coach Thomson's leadership, Shoreline has twice won the State Community College championship and has had three state pole vault champions in the past eight years.*

There are three things that make a successful pole vaulter. I believe they come in the following order: (1) equipment and conditions; (2) training; and (3) technique. This is the way we teach the pole vault to our boys at Shoreline. We have found it to be an extremely successful method.

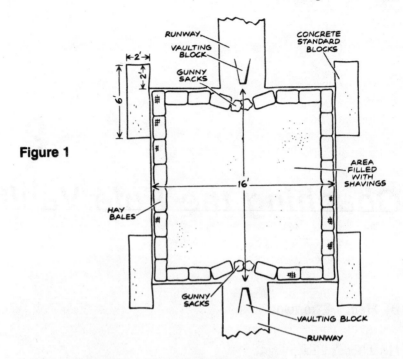

Figure 1

EQUIPMENT

The Vaulting Area: The first thing that any novice vaulter has to do is to overcome his fear of a hard landing and possible injury. This is a must, because if he doesn't, all the techniques and training methods that the coach can devise will be meaningless. The boys must think *only* of clearing the bar to be successful. In order to allow the vaulter to concentrate on his vaulting, the coach must eliminate the root of the fear. The way to do this is through construction of a pit area that will make the landing as safe and as comfortable as possible. We feel we have built just such a pit area at Shoreline. Here is how you can build one.

The first thing to do is to dig up an area 16 feet wide by 16 feet long by 1 foot deep. Fill the pit with old bed springs (you can usually get these at a local junkyard). Cover the springs with plywood and then surround the pit with straw bales, leaving an opening at both sides in front of the vaulting boxes as illustrated in Figure 1. It is a good idea to put a gunny sack or two in front of these openings to prevent the shavings from getting outside the pit. After all this has been done, fill the pit with approximately 20 yards of shavings. The shavings should reach about 6 to 7 feet above the pit, and, combined with the give of the springs, will produce a comfortable landing even from heights of 14 to 15 feet.

> FOAM: I know that the use of foam rubber is best for the pit. The cost, however, is usually too much for the average high school's athletic budget.

On both sides of our pit, we have runways and vaulting boxes so that the athletes can vault in either direction. The runways are made of rubberized asphalt and are approximately 140 feet long. We have found this to be a surface that is easy to run on, resists wear, and is especially valuable in places where there is a lot of rainfall. It is also a runway that maintains its characteristics under all conditions. This gives the vaulter confidence because he knows that once he has established his take-off point, he will hit it every time. He is able, therefore, to concentrate on the techniques of his vault rather than continually running through his marks.

Poles: As far as the vaulting poles are concerned, we have two ideas that we try to follow. First, we try to keep a stock of as many sizes and kinds of poles as is possible. This can be pretty expensive, but the more poles you have to choose from, the more likely you are to fit your boys with the right ones. Second, I *insist* that all of our beginning vaulters learn on the steel pole before switching to the fiberglass pole.

> STEEL POLE: I firmly believe that it is easier to teach the novice vaulter on the stiffer pole. The steel pole, because it is stiffer than the glass one, allows the boy more control. And control is a must if an athlete is to learn correct vaulting techniques.

TRAINING

Off-Season Training: Pole vaulting, like the majority of field events, is becoming so specialized and competitive that it requires year 'round attention. I believe that gymnastic training is extremely valuable to the pole vaulter. Work on the trampoline teaches the athlete control of his body. Work on the rings, ropes, horizontal and parallel bars also aids in building body coordination while building the arm and shoulder strength so necessary to the vaulter.

RECRUITS: I have gotten the greatest majority of my vault-ers from our gymnastic program. If your school has such a program, you might consider it a good place to look for your recruits. Remember, most gymnasts possess many of the physical qualities of good vaulters.

Early-Season Training: During the first week of the season, our vaulters spend their time working out with the rest of the track team on the cross-country course. They also participate in our early season decathlon competition. We run one or two events each day for the first week-and-a-half of the season. The events are the 75, 300, 440, 880, 120 low hurdles, shot put, high jump, running broad jump and cross-country. We run the decathlon for the following three reasons: (1) it shows the coaches in what event our athletes are most proficient and often uncovers hidden talent or a second event in one or more of the boys; (2) it is a good conditioning program that the boys *enjoy*; and (3) it acts as a motivating force because each boy tries to accumulate as many points as he can.

MOTIVATION: As an added incentive, we post a "Big Ten" list on the school bulletin board after each event is com-pleted. We also award a "Spike Shoe Pin" to all athletes reaching a certain minimum point total in the decathlon. The boys on the track squad consider it quite an honor to be a member of the "Spike Shoe Club."

While we are carrying on the decathlon, we also have our vault-ers working on their run. The majority of our early practice time is spent on developing the proper steps in our vaulters. We also train them in hurdling, and they run a great many 70-yard low hurdles with the hurdles set 10 yards apart and 120-yard low hurdles with the hurdles 20 yards apart. I believe that hurdling is one of the best things to teach a vaulter uniformity of stride and consistency during the ap-proach run.

SMALL STAFF: Since we have a small staff, we leave much of the coaching to an appointed event leader who is usually one of the senior vaulters. We plan the daily schedule for the vaulters, and the event leader meets with them after squad calisthenics and explains and demonstrates the work to be done.

GENERAL VAULTING TECHNIQUES

The most important part of the vault is the beginning. If the vaulter does not accomplish this initial phase correctly, all the rest will suffer.

The Run: The first necessity is a proper run. When the boy gains confidence that his pole placement will be correct, he will be able to concentrate on proper technique. Here at Shoreline, we use a trial and error method of working out our steps. We start the run at a spot 110 to 120 feet from the box and keep working on the run until the athlete feels he has the proper steps. Only then do we measure and set up a mark for the vaulter. Each boy works many hours on his steps early in the season. He continually revises his starting mark as his speed increases during the season.

ONE MARK: We use only one mark for our vaulters. We place this very near the start of the run because we feel that by using more than one mark, we would make the vaulter worry too much about his marks rather than concentrating on his pole plant and initial swing.

The Pole Plant: I always insist on an early plant. One of my "favorite" coaching phrases is, "You are planting your pole too late." When the pole is planted, it must be brought to an overhead position as close to the body as possible and directly over and in front of the boy as he starts.

"One and Two": After the vaulter has planted his pole, we have him use our "one and two" count. At "One," the right-handed vaulter jabs his left heel in the runway and thrusts his right knee directly up. We provide all our vaulters with heel cups for their planting foot. The "two" count occurs early during the swing. It is where the vaulter must drop his right leg even with the left one so that he will get a smoother and better swing.

Hip Position: During the pull up, the most common fault is bringing the hips too high. Bring the legs up, but keep the hips low.

The Release: The coach must remind his vaulters to remain on the pole until it reaches the perpendicular. He must also make sure that they release with their bottom hand first. Many young vaulters who go over the crossbar on their back or side do so because they release with their top hand first.

3

Coaching Champion High Jumpers

by Howard Bagwell

Head Track Coach
Baptist (Charleston, South Carolina) College

Howard Bagwell has been coaching high school and college track for the past 23 years. His 14-year record in South Carolina high schools is 139-13 and includes 6 state championships and 3 state runner-ups. His 9-year record at Baptist College is 64-12 and includes 3 state championships (only 4 held) and 1 state runner-up.

Before you can develop the champion high jumper, you need some method of determining the potentially good high jumpers—the boys with some natural ability.

JUMP AND REACH TEST: Toward this end, we give all physical education students the jump and reach test. The boy stands adjacent to a wall and marks his upward reach from a normal standing position. He then jumps as high as possible and places a mark at this point.

If the difference between the standing and jumping marks is 23 or more inches, you have an excellent high jumping prospect. Here's the way we develop such a prospect into a champion.

Exercises: Leg spring is hereditary to some extent, but it can be improved with hard work. We use weights for this purpose. The specific exercises we stress are half squats, toe raises and leg presses.

1. Half squats are done by getting under the weights, which are supported by a rack, and raising them—and going up on the toes as high as possible. Half squats are used rather than full squats because they can be repeated much faster.

2. Toe raises are performed by getting under the weights and raising on the toes as high as possible. This exercise gives one the same heel and toe action as when high jumping.

3. Leg presses are executed while lying on the back under the weight and pushing the bar upwards with the feet.

AMOUNT OF WEIGHT: The amount of weight is determined by the size and the strength of each boy. Naturally, more weights are added as the boy progresses.

We lift three days a week. To a lesser degree, we also work with weights on the upper part of the body. Exercises used here are the press, arm curls and sit-ups with the weight on the chest.

Beginning High Jumpers: We start off our beginning high jumpers by placing a crossbar about one foot above the ground—and teaching the boy to land with both hands and his right foot at the same time (assuming the boy jumps from the left side). As the bar is moved higher, he will begin to land more on his right side—and finally, on his back. It's important that the pits have a soft surface to prevent the boy from landing like a cat—on his feet.

STRADDLE ROLL: We teach all jumpers the straddle roll (and no other) for two reasons: (1) I'm convinced that it's the best; (2) it's important that all jumpers use the same form as they learn much from observing each other.

It must be understood that boys are going to learn in sequential experiences. They are not going to jump higher and higher each day—no matter how hard they work. They will level off and may even recede some. Then, all of a sudden, they will spurt forward again. If boys are told that this is how they will learn, they will not be discouraged when they remain on one plateau for a time. Of course, these plateaus are not the same length for all boys.

OTHER FACTORS: The amount of work and desire on each boy's part determines the individual learning pattern. On the average, it becomes such a consistent factor that we schedule our weak and strong meets according to it.

High Jumping Techniques: The following techniques are emphasized to our high jumpers:

1. *Proper distance from the bar on take-off.* Many jumpers take off too far from the bar. Generally, an arm's length perpendicular from the bar is the proper distance. Taking off too far from the bar will result in too much effort going forward instead of up. Also, the height of one's jump may be reached before getting over the bar—and the bar may be knocked off coming down.

2. *Angle of approach.* We use the seven-step approach from a 45-degree angle. If the angle is less than 45 degrees, it becomes more difficult to get the legs over soon enough. The first four steps are used to build up speed, and that speed is maintained during the last three strides. It is important that the foot be in line with the run so as not to start the roll prematurely while still on the ground.

3. *The take-off.* The foot should be planted with the heel first and the last stride lengthened. This is to check the forward motion and transfer it to an upward motion. During this step, the upper body should be tilted back as far as possible—also, the trailing leg swung through as much as possible. This lengthens the lever, and therefore increases the amount of momentum at the end of the kick. The kick should be slightly at an angle toward the bar to initiate the roll. The opposite arm is thrown up as vigorously as the kick is executed, which eliminates dropping the shoulder into the bar.

4. *Action on top of the bar.* On top of the bar, the trail leg should be lifted and the foot turned to the outside. This action helps the trail leg to clear the bar. The jumper should attempt to roll his lead arm and knee back underneath the bar as he starts his downward movement.

COMMON FAULTS: (1) Upper torso over bar too much ahead of the rest of the body; (2) jumper does not lean back enough on last step before leaving the ground; (3) jumper's lead leg not straight; (4) jumper kicks trail leg on top of the bar rather than lifting it; (5) dipping shoulder into bar on upward flight.

The "Western Dive" in High Jumping

by Frank Zubovich

Assistant Track Coach
Ohio State University

Frank Zubovich has been coaching track and field on the high school and college levels since 1957. At Glenville (Cleveland, Ohio) High School, he compiled a dual meet record of 41 wins, 9 losses and 1 tie. In state competition, his squads captured the championship 3 times, and placed second twice. At present, he is assistant track coach at Ohio State University.

The average individual who attempts to learn the technique of high jumping will ultimately realize that there's no simple way of determining which style will suit him best.

NOTE: To acquire a method that enables a jumper to utilize his mental and physical capabilities, one should begin simply on a trial and error basis—keeping in mind the basics of the jump.

Here are some considerations in this respect.

THE STRADDLE STYLE

Most coaches feel that the straddle style of jumping is the most effective and begin by teaching this form. However, in many cases, the individual does not have the ability to coordinate the movements necessary to perform the jump.

COMMON FAULT: One common fault of the straddle jumper, especially the novice, is the tendency to anticipate the take-off by turning or leaning into the cross bar.

Many straddle jumpers are guilty of this—and it's a constant battle for the jumper to control this anxiety for early lay-out. Whereas most good jumpers use the straddle form, there seems to be an emergence of top-flight jumpers who are employing effectively the Western style of clearance.

THE WESTERN DIVE

For the individual who has good spring but poor adaptability to the straddle jump, there is the possibility of his utilizing effectively the Western dive form of jumping. It is simply a Western roll with greater emphasis placed on modifying the clearance so as to get the hips up and out of the way quickly as the cross bar is cleared.

BASIC COMPONENTS: Like other methods of high jumping, the basic components of the Western dive include the approach, the take-off and clearance.

These can be defined as separate parts. However, the position from one part to another must be a coordinated fluid action, with the success of the jump dependent upon accurate calculations during each phase of the jump in succession.

Approach: The approach to the take-off, which includes the length and speed of run and angle of approach, will vary with each individual. The factor governing the adequacy of the approach is simply whether or not it puts the jumper in proper position and attitude for take-off. We generally start our Western roll jumpers with an eight-step approach at an angle of 45 to 50 degrees. With this wide angle there is a reduced tendency to lean toward the cross bar. After the jumper gains confidence in his ability to take off without leaning, the angle can be reduced slightly.

STEPS: The first two steps of the approach are walking steps. The next six are running strides, with each stride progressively faster and longer to the point of take-off. The last two strides are extremely important, for it is with these strides that the center of gravity is lowered and a backward lean effected. This is done to get the body in the proper latitude for take-off.

As the cross bar is raised to heights above the jumper's head, the tendency will be to take off farther away from the pit. For this reason it is important for the jumper to have practiced his approach a sufficient number of times in order to hit his take-off spot accurately no matter to which height the bar is raised.

Take-Off: As the jumper reaches his take-off spot, he strikes it firmly with his left foot and almost simultaneously swings the right leg upward. At the same time, the arms are swung upward vigorously. The spring from the ground is executed when the jumper rocks up on the toes and the body weight passes above the take-off foot.

SPRING: Most experts agree that speed in the execution of the spring is extremely important and that there is a definite relationship between speed of spring and height of jump.

As the jumper leaves the ground, flexion on the left leg occurs with the right leg remaining relatively straight. During the course of this phase of the jump, the objective is to swing the right leg high and to tuck the bent left leg as near to the trunk as possible. The timing of the left leg tuck along with the right leg swing initiates rotation of the body.

Clearance: The jumper is ready for clearance when his body reaches its highest point. As a result of the high swing of the right leg and a quick tuck of the left leg firmly toward the trunk, the hips are raised. At this point, the head and shoulders are dropped downward toward the pit. The left arm is thrust downward and the right arm swung to the right—thus providing added impetus to the dive toward the pit.

NOTE: Providing various movements connected with the jump have been properly coordinated, the momentum of the run will carry the jumper across the bar.

In the Western roll, the actual landing is accomplished by absorbing the shock with the arms and right leg. But in many cases, the jump is such that the jumper may roll completely over prior to hitting the pit. Any landing that minimizes the danger of injury is acceptable.

SUMMARY: The role of every high jumper should be to master a specific technique of jumping. To be a champion takes coordination, strength, agility and spring. The mental factors—desire to excel, competitive spirit and the ability to utilize jumping knowledge—also play important parts.

5

Teaching the "Fosbury Flop" to High Jumpers

by Doug Hyke

Head Track Coach
Havre (Montana) High School

Douglas Hyke had been head track coach at Havre High School for the past 13 years, where his squads have a 89% winning record in dual and triangular meets. During that time his teams have won 25 major Invitational Meets, 4 State Championships and 4 Eastern Montana Divisional Championships. Coach Hyke was named Montana Class A Coach-of-the-Year 4 times.

We started teaching the "fosbury flop" to our high jumpers three years ago and found it much simpler to teach and master than the straddle roll.

NOTE: The straddle roll creates problems with the arms, and especially the trail leg. It is much easier to get the width of the body over the bar with the fosbury flop, compared to the entire body length with the straddle roll.

Can you easily convert a straddle jumper to the fosbury flop? The answer is yes. Most jumpers can convert in a few weeks. One of our jumpers made the conversion in just two weeks and went on to win the state championship in the high jump.

LITTLE PRACTICE, NO DANGER

Another advantage of the fosbury flop is that after you master the technique, very little jumping practice is necessary. Once or twice a week is sufficient. Our best high jumper, who cleared 6' 9", worked out just once a week.

Is the fosbury flop dangerous? The answer is no—as long as you have a good foam rubber landing pit. Pole vaulters have been landing on their backs and shoulders from much greater heights for years with no serious injury.

IMPORTANT: An important point to remember is that with the fosbury flop, your center of gravity is lower than with any other high jumping style. Therefore, a jumper uses less energy in getting over a given height.

EXECUTION

As the jumper approaches the bar for the take-off, his hips will be lowered into a crouch position. His heel strikes the ground first (Figure 1), and then he completes a rock-up on his toes. There is a backward lean of the body as the take-off foot is planted. The left leg is extended at the same time as the right knee is driven up across the body. The right and left arms are driven up to give lift to the jumper (Figures 2, 3, and 4).

The hips and shoulders are rotated to the left as the jumper takes off. The trunk will be rotated about 100°. The angle of approach to the bar will be above 70° (Figures 4 and 5). The arms are now held along the side of the body.

The lay-back begins before the turn is half finished (Figures 5 and 6). The head is turned to the right as one clears the bar. The eyes have been focused on the bar since the start of the jump. The jumper's arms are held alongside of the body (Figures 6 and 7).

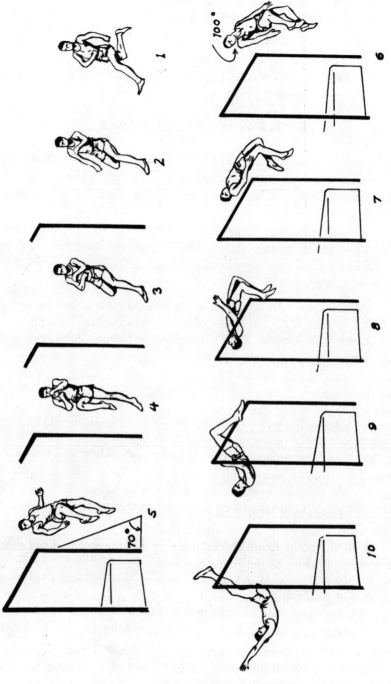

Figures 1-10

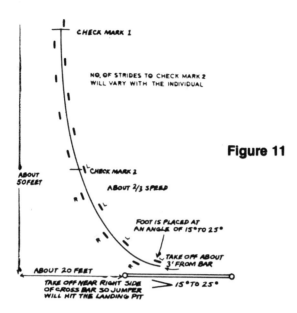

CHECK MARK 1

NO. OF STRIDES TO CHECK MARK 2
WILL VARY WITH THE INDIVIDUAL

Figure 11

ABOUT
50 FEET

CHECK MARK 2

ABOUT 2/3 SPEED

FOOT IS PLACED AT
AN ANGLE OF 15° TO 25°

TAKE OFF ABOUT
3' FROM BAR

ABOUT 20 FEET

TAKE OFF NEAR RIGHT SIDE
OF CROSS BAR SO JUMPER
WILL HIT THE LANDING PIT

15° TO 25°

NOTE: The jumper must be careful not to lower the arms at this point as he will displace the cross bar.

When the turn is complete, the shoulders are parallel to the bar and the legs are still flexed (Figure 8). When the shoulders reach the bar, the jumper will drop his head slightly and arch his back. This will raise the hips to clear the bar.

As soon as the hips cross the bar, the legs are flipped to clear the bar (Figures 9 and 10). As the bar is cleared, the hips are dropped and the arms are raised (Figure 10). This will stop further rotation and allow the jumper to land on his shoulders.

APPROACH RUN FOR RIGHT-HANDED JUMPERS

Start at a point about 20 feet to the right of the standard and about 50 feet out in front of the right standard (Figure 11). A minimum of seven curved strides are taken from check mark number 2. The run begins in a direction perpendicular to the bar and then curves toward it from the right side.

The last step brings you into the bar at an angle of about 200 degrees and about 3 feet away from the bar. Speed of approach should be fast—about two-thirds of one's top speed. The number of total strides taken is a matter of personal taste.

Part VIII

Broad Jump,* Triple Jump

* The editors of *The Coaching Clinic* wish to acknowledge that the obsolete term *broad jump* has been used in the following articles, rather than the current term *long jump,* in order to maintain the integrity of the articles as they were originally written and published in *The Coaching Clinic*.

1

Developing the High School Broad Jumper

by Steve Hansen

Head Track Coach
Woodland (Washington) High School

> *Steve Hansen has been coaching high school track for 15 years. As head track coach at Woodland High School, he has produced 2 state championship 880 relay teams and set a new state record. He has also seen his share of district and individual championships—two district crowns and a second place; six individual state champions.*

Candidates for the broad jump must possess some running and jumping ability before they may be considered as serious contenders in this event. When you find both of these qualities in the same boy, you have a potentially great broad jumper. With such a boy, we stress the following techniques for developing his potential.

THE RUN: The high school broad jumper must run 110 to 120 feet. The more mature boy may run even farther. But without a run of at least this length, the boy does not allow himself enough distance to build up the speed needed for the jump.

Check Marks: The setting of check marks is most important. The stride plan may vary as to the exact setting, but the standardization of the stride on the marks cannot vary. As a matter of fact, the marks must be checked daily. As the jumper becomes better conditioned, his stride is likely to change slightly. When setting the check marks, it is best to work on a lane of the track that has been brushed to remove all foot prints. In the following discussion, we'll assume that the jumper uses a left-foot take off and that the approach will be with 2-8-12 stride plan.

Stride Plan: The jumper starts with his toes on a specific starting point. Starting with the right foot, he jogs out *two easy strides* and repeats this until the left foot hits the first check mark the same each time. When these two strides have become standardized, he keeps working down the runway at two-thirds effort to the second check mark, which is *eight strides away.* He should run through these two check marks until the toe of the left foot can hit the marks consistently. After hitting the second check mark, he starts to accelerate to seven-eights effort for the third check mark *(twelve strides away)* and the take-off board (see Diagram 1). The jumper should repeat this approach until he can hit all three of his check marks consistently.

FINAL ADJUSTMENTS: Now that the check marks have been set and the stride has been standardized, measure carefully all of the marks, including the point where the jumper stands before starting. Then take the measured marks to the broad jump runway and set them on it. The check marks should now place the take-off foot on the take-off board. Take several practice runs to make any final adjustments.

Even Stride: In order for these, or any other, check marks to work for the broad jumper, he must have an even stride. Working on a flight of low hurdles is one of the best ways to develop this even stride; without it, you can't hit the hurdles correctly.

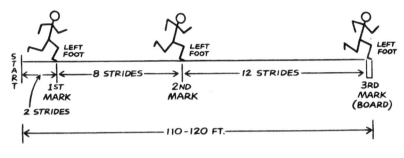

Diagram 1

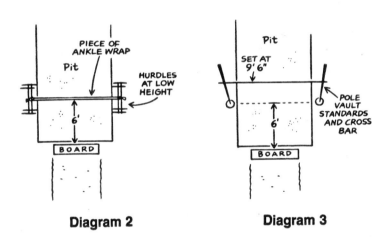

Diagram 2   **Diagram 3**

During the last three strides the jumper must "gather" slightly for the proper foot plant and take-off. The last stride should be shortened a bit so that he can convert his speed and momentum upward rather than out. If he hits the board at top speed, he may have trouble making this conversion.

The foot plant itself should be a heel-toe action. The heel of the take-off foot will land first, followed by a rock-up onto the toe. The take-off leg should be relatively straight, and the body weight should be centered over the take-off foot.

Height: The boy must remember that he is jumping up first, then out. As he leaves the take-off board, both hands should be thrust upward. The opposite leg must also be driven up, with the knee leading the action. This in itself will help attain the needed height.

IMPORTANT POINT: Keep in mind that if the boy's hips are flexed, it will bring his tail down. Have him try to avoid hip flexion as long as possible.

Another point we stress is the paddling of the arms backward as the flight in the air is ending. This, too, can add precious inches. After the arms have been pulled back, they must also come forward as soon as the boy has landed. This will help to get his body going forward and keep him from falling backward. When landing, the feet must be forward, and the jumper must telescope his body forward. A good way to develop the proper arm swing is to work on the standing broad jump with dumbbells.

TWO TECHNIQUES: Here are two techniques we stress to help the jumper attain a maximum height—(1) the "soft hurdles" and (2) the use of pole vault standards with a cross-bar.

1. By "soft hurdles" I mean that we place a hurdle on each side of the runway about six feet past the take-off board. An ankle wrap is stretched between them (see Diagram 2). The hurdle is set at low hurdle height, and the jumper must get up in the air to get over the wrap.

2. The use of the pole vault standards and cross-bar is much the same. We place the standards on the sides of the runway about six feet past the board. The cross-bar is set at 9 feet 6 inches as a starting point (see Diagram 3). The jumper, working on form, is trying to get his hands up to the cross-bar. This helps him get his whole body in the air.

NOTE: We want the hands thrust upward. This drill will make the jumper get his hands up as well as force him to jump up rather than out. As the jumper develops the skill of getting height, the cross-bar can be raised.

Other Techniques: We also stress the following points as aids for developing the high school broad jumper:

1. The "pop-up"—the last three strides of the approach stressing the dip and lift—is an excellent training device. For a left-footed jumper this would be left, right, left—pop. By using the "pop-up" a boy can work for a long period of time on his foot plant, height, action

in the air and the landing. Pops can be done on the grass as a means of warming up.

2. In addition to having a regular check mark, I feel that a short mark is needed. That is, one at something less than half of the regular run. This short run should be used for almost all of the jumping done in practice. All of the training devices discussed should be used with the short run.

3. Running, of course, is most important. Since broad jumpers generally double as sprinters or hurdlers, their running programs are the same as those events. Thus, their conditioning comes with running workouts, leaving the jumping workouts for form and technique.

4. To add fun to our training program, we have our boys "play with" the hop, step and jump (triple jump). Our jumpers find this very enjoyable as well as an aid to their event.

5. During the off-season, we have our jumpers work with the weights. The weight training program is two-fold in nature: (1) a general body-building program, and (2) to correct or develop any particular weakness in the boy.

2

Isometrics and Step Running for Broad Jumpers

by Gene Cox

Head Track Coach
Pratt (Kansas) Junior College

Gene Cox has been coaching track and football at both the high school and junior college level for the past 13 years. At Bonner Springs (Kansas) High School, his track squads captured all-state honors in the pole vault, shot put, 220 and broad jump over a 5-year period. Presently at Pratt (Kansas) Junior College, he has had a national champion in the 100-yard dash and placed second in the 220.

While head track coach at Bonner Springs (Kansas) High School in the spring of 1963, it was my pleasure to coach one of our broad jumpers, Frank Jones, who won the Class A state track meet with a jump of 23′ 7¼″. This jump set a new state record in Class A competition. Frank was a junior at the time, 5′ 10″ and weighing 155 pounds.

SUCCESS: Although there are a number of factors involved in a successful broad jump, I believe the primary factor in Frank's success was his isometric and step-running work in the pre-season.

In 1962, Frank's best jump was 21′ 2″, and he achieved this only once. Most of his jumps for the season were in the 20′ range. His consistent 22′ jump in 1963 and his record 23′ 7¼″ jump in the state track meet represent an exceptional progress for one year. I feel that the following isometric and step-running exercises contributed greatly to his improvement:

ISOMETRICS

1. *Lift-up:* overhand grip, arms bent, knees bent (Figure 1). Maximum contraction on arms, legs and back: 8 seconds.
2. *Push-up:* put bar at head level, arms bent, knees bent (Figure 2). Maximum contraction on arms, shoulders, back and legs: 8 seconds.
3. *Push-out:* arms and legs bent, palms pressed against sides (Figure 3). Maximum contraction on arms, shoulders and back: 8 seconds.
4. *Pull-in:* hands around side bars with arms slightly bent (Figure 4). Maximum contraction on shoulders and chest: 8 seconds.
5. *Shoulder-lift:* knees bent, arms bent, bar resting on back of neck (Figure 5). Maximum contraction on arms, back and legs: 8 seconds.
6. *Leg-push:* lie on back, legs bent, hands braced against side bars (Figure 6). Maximum extension with legs: 8 seconds.

STEP RUNNING

1. Run approximately 200 steps, up and down, daily.
2. Go slow—exaggerate pushing off of toes and getting complete leg extension with each step.
3. When going down steps, let the full weight of the body shift to each leg.
4. Do not skip any step—hit every one.

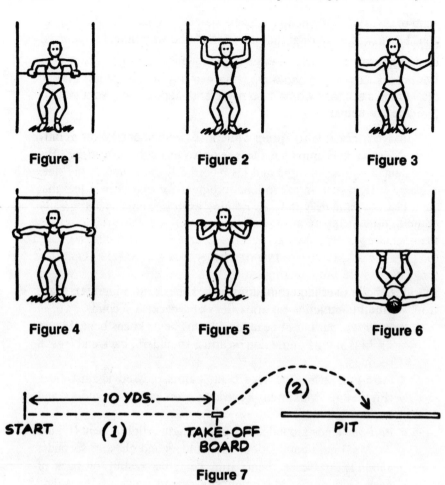

Figure 1   Figure 2   Figure 3

Figure 4   Figure 5   Figure 6

Figure 7

NOTE: Other factors involved in Frank's success included
(1) good leg strength; (2) good competitor; (3) good sense of
timing and rhythm, which was a big asset particularly in the
last few steps prior to jumping.

Although most good broad jumpers have good sprint speed,
Frank's best time in the 100-yard dash was only 10.5; therefore, he had
to rely on leg strength and rhythm rather than on speed. His work in the
low hurdles and the 440-yard dash probably helped develop his legs
and stride.

We worked a fair amount of the time on the boy's step, an easy thing for him to ''get'' because of his hurdle background (he was used to maintaining a stride). We used the double check point method in finding his step and stride marks. Frank never did a lot of jumping for distance, particularly within three days of a meet; he worked instead on jumping for height (Figure 7).

1. Run only at ½ to ¾ speed (do not worry about take-off point).
2. Try to gain maximum height—also use arms in getting lift.

NOTE: We did 10 to 15 of these per day.

The jumping style is what I call a lay-out style. Shortly after the takeoff, the hips go in advance of the shoulders and the legs trail. At the beginning of the down approach, the hips are whipped forward and the arms are outstretched forward. The legs are held up and forward as long as possbile until landing in the pit. We feel that this hip whip action is another aid in getting distance as it helps throw the feet out in front a little farther.

3

Doubling in the Broad and Triple Jumps

by Dr. L. T. Walker

Head Track Coach
North Carolina (Durham, North Carolina) Central University

Dr. Leroy T. Walker has a lifetime record to date of 65 wins and losses in dual and triangular competition. He has received many honors during his illustrious career–among others, the Helms Hall of Fame and the NAIA National Coach of the Year Award. Dr. Walker is the holder of numerous individual honors and the author of three books and various articles on track and field.

If you are using your broad jumpers to "double" in the triple jump, note these basic points:

1. The body lean at takeoff is more pronounced in the triple jump than it is in the broad jump (Diagrams 1a and 1b).

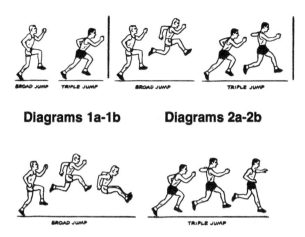

Diagrams 1a-1b   Diagrams 2a-2b

Diagrams 3a-3b

CAUTION: The triple jumper should not increase forward body lean to a degree which prevents a smooth, synchronized elevation of the free leg.

2. The takeoff (for the hop) is executed low with minimum elevation, head up and eyes focused forward. This is contrasted with the upward lift of the broad jump (Diagrams 2a and 2b).

3. The body position and elevation changes in each flight of the triple jump in contrast to the single body flight attitude of the broad jump. The changes in the triple are from a forward lean at takeoff (the hop), to a nearly erect position in the step, to an erect position in the jump. With each increase in height, careful attention must be given to sustaining the forward momentum.

4. The triple jumper must master a synchronized bending and unbending of the knees in the three flights as compared to the single action of the broad jump (Diagrams 3a and 3b).

5. The distance factor in the triple jump is influenced by the execution of three distinct flights instead of one. The "Step" flight is the one that most often requires lengthening. The flight distance, however, that must be increased will be determined by the jumper's complete pattern. The pattern often varies even when the total distance is the same.

4

Coaching the Triple Jump

by Dr. Martin Pushkin

Assistant Professor of Health and Physical Education
Virginia Polytechnic (Blacksburg, Virginia) Institute

Dr. Martin Pushkin had only one losing season in ten years of coaching track and cross country at VPI. His teams won 30 of the last 32 dual meets in track and field and his hurdle teams have always been outstanding. At present, he is a full-time assistant professor of health and physical education.

The triple jump is finally gaining the acceptance it needs and deserves in becoming an integral part of the track and field program. Although accepted by the NCAA, there are many high schools which still do not include the hop, step, and jump in their program. Its challenge is so great that it may someday outmode the long jump altogether.

TERMINOLOGY: The use of the term "hop, step, and jump" is misleading, and is technically incorrect. The German terminology *drei sprung* or "triple jump" is far more correct. The triple jump is three successive jumps—the first two off the same leg and the third off the other; there is no step involved.

Essential Qualities: To be a top performer in the triple jump, the four qualities most needed are speed, jumping ability, strength in the related muscles, and skill. It was initially felt that the shock of landing and the energy required for leaping were too great to allow for top speed in this event. However, with the advent of regular weight training programs for track and field, this premise no longer holds true.

NOTE: Related strength training can and does strengthen the leg muscles, tendons, and ligaments, to the point where they can withstand great stress.

Secondly, best performance calls for great jumping ability. One's best potential triple jump should be equal to 75 per cent of one's best broad jump—20' x 3 x .75= 45'.

Thirdly, best performance requires great strength and resiliency in the related muscles which must absorb the body weight as it lands from the three successive phases of the triple jump. During the final phase, the muscles must react with enough force to thrust the body up into the air with minimum loss of momentum.

NOTE: Finally, best performance in the triple jump requires great skill. Like the pole vaulter or the discus thrower, the triple jumper must master the basic skills early and practice them at length in order to achieve high level performance.

Approach Run: The approach run in the triple run is distinctively different from that of the broad jump. The runner must remain relaxed and not accelerate to the point where control is sacrificed at the expense of speed. Speed is important but it must be controlled speed. Control depends upon a relaxed approach, good balance at the time of the takeoff, and proper body alignment throughout all three phases of the jump.

No phase of the jump should be rushed and the jumper should jump as hard as possible only on the last jump. It must be emphasized that relaxed speed is an essential ingredient in the approach. The jumper must have his center of gravity directly over or slightly ahead of his takeoff foot—and this is accomplished by a slight settling of the body during the last three of four steps prior to takeoff.

TIP: The jumper should not rear back and plant the heel as is done in the broad jump.

First Phase: The first phase of the triple jump should be kept as low as possible. This will detract from the loss of forward momentum which is essential in carrying out the remainder of the jump. The jumper should have a definite mark for which to aim. The free leg is thrust out and forward, keeping the jumper close to the ground. The landing foot must not be too far ahead of the body or the jumper will collapse as the foot hits the ground, or be forced into a quick, short step.

NOTE: During the carry from the takeoff board, the jumper should keep his body tilted forward from the hips up and hold his chest in an upright position. The arms should be used for balance and work in conjunction with the legs in creating forward thrust. The head should not drop down and the eyes should be focused on the predesignated mark of touch-down.

Arm Action: This action should be much like the action of the breast stroke in swimming. The forward, upward thrust of the arms should be coordinated with the drive of the free leg. The jumper should give the appearance of swimming through the air to the ground. He should maintain this high leg position and not hurry to get the foot down. If the jumper "waits out" this high leg position, he will be in a better position when the foot lands prior to the final phase. Just before landing, the jumper forcefully extends his leading leg.

Final Jump: The final jump is similar to the broad jump. The jumper should drive from the heel up and over the toe. Leg thrust should be upward and the head should be thrown back to facilitate a gain in height. Maximum effort should be utilized during the third phase.

NOTE: The triple jump requires great leg strength, and this must be developed through a regular program of weight training, running steps, and jumping alternately off both legs. Speed is essential and should be improved upon—but remember that control is never sacrificed at the expense of speed.

5

The Triple Jump in High School Track

by John Arcaro

Head Track Coach
Baldwinsville (New York) Academy

John Arcaro's record as head track at Baldwinsville Academy is 189 wins and 16 losses in dual meets. His teams have won the O.H.S.L. championship 14 of the last 20 years and have also won various Invitational Meets.

The triple jump has been one of our poorest events in International competition. Part of the poor showing is possibly due to the fact that it has only been about five years since high schools have added this event to their track and field programs. Not too many years ago, 46 feet was a good triple jump for most college competitors. However, with more boys taking part in this event, the distance has improved.

NOTE: Art Foster, who is the leading United States triple jumper, jumps 52 feet plus—and has a good chance to be the first American to win the Olympics in this event.

Here are some ideas and techniques to help you improve the triple jump in your track program.

RULES FOR THE TRIPLE JUMP

1. A triple jumper must take off with his hop from a board which is level with the runway. The board is usually 32 feet or more from the pit. He must land next on the same foot on which he hopped. He then goes into his step and must come down on the opposite foot. From this foot he takes off for his jump, and the rest is the same as the long jump.

2. If the jumper drags or touches his trailing foot to the ground while he is finishing his hop or his step, the jump is classified a foul.

3. Each competitor is allowed from 3 to 6 trial jumps, and the top 5 competitors will get 3 more final jumps. The person with the longest jump in the trials will go last, and so forth. In some of the bigger meets, they will draw for position in the finals. If a competitor has a longer jump in the finals, this will be credited as his best. His trial jump can get him a place even though he didn't have a better jump in the finals.

4. The approach run that a competitor takes can be of any distance. He can place marks on the runway to adjust for his steps.

5. You measure the jump from the nearest break in the pit closest to the scratch line or takeoff line. The distance should be measured to the nearest ¼ inch.

6. The board you take off from should be placed solidly in the ground 32 feet or more from the jumping pit. It should be painted white and made of wood. On the new all-weather tracks, the board is usually painted white on the surface. The board should be 4 feet long and 8 inches wide.

NOTE: All other rules concerning this event are the same as the long jump.

FOR BETTER JUMPING CONDITIONS

1. A well-packed level runway made of cinders, clay or the all-weather surface material is a must. The runway should be at least 135 feet.

2. The ground between the takeoff board and pit should be from 8 to 10 feet wide and must be level. We found that grass works well. Other tracks have the same type of surface as their runways.

PIT: The pit should be made as soft as possible because of the hard pounding in landing. Sawdust mixed with sand and fine dirt works very well. For the best break, the mixture should be moistened before competition.

3. The competitor should wear heel cups or some type of sponge heel to protect himself from the constant pounding on his foot. Many good triple jumpers hurt their heels and are out of competition for several weeks.

SELECTING THE TRIPLE JUMPER

The competitor must realize that the triple jump puts tremendous strain on the whole body. Conditioning for this event has to be much greater than for other events in track and field.

1. The triple jumper must have strong upper and lower legs.
2. He must have better-than-average speed and it must be controlled.
3. Coordination is a must for the triple jumper.
4. A good height for a boy would be from 5′8″ to 5′11″.
5. Ideal weight would be from 135 pounds to 150 pounds. This is not a set rule—but boys of this weight just seem to jump better for us.
6. Being a good long jumper sometimes helps.

NOTE: We look for the freshman or the younger boy because it takes a few years to master this event. Test your high and low hurdlers for prospects—this is the type of skill needed. It will not always be true that an outstanding triple jumper will make a good long jumper.

TRAINING FOR THE TRIPLE JUMP

In the off-season, the triple jumper should be on the weights and on general conditioning exercises. We stress a lot of rope jumping, hopping, and striding. Short sprints and hurdling have been musts for our triple jumpers. In the past few seasons, we have used circuit training for this event.

CIRCUIT TRAINING: In our method, we use 5 exercises for the circuit: (1) straddle jump; (2) step-ups; (3) V-sit-ups; (4) hopping 2 times on one foot then 2 times on the other foot; (5) 50-foot run on the exer-geni ropes.

We test each exercise for 1 minute—seeing how many times it can be done in this time. The testing will take each boy 5 minutes. After you know the number done for each exercise, you cut the number in half.

EXAMPLE: A boy does 50 step-ups in 1 minute; his work load for this exercise would be 25 step-ups. This is done for all 5 exercises. We separate the stations so that the boy will have to run to get to them. The boy has 5 minutes to do his work load of the 5 exercises as many times as he can. As soon as he can do the 5 exercises 3 times in order in 5 minutes, the work load must be changed—so you retest the boy.

SPEED PLAY

For our speed play, we use an area which is approximately 3 miles in length, and perform the following: (a) a 70-second 440-yard run; (b) boy scout drill (run 50 yards, walk 50 yards for 440 yards; (c) hop 50 yards with the right foot and repeat with the left foot; (d) 110-yard sprint and jog 110 yards (perform for 440 yards); (e) stride for 150 yards, fast walking for 150 yards (perform for 880 yards).

We have the boy repeat the drill as many times as he feels he is conditioned for. Following are some of the training methods we employ in our weekly workouts for the triple jump. We use 3 or 4 each night depending upon the triple jumper's work progress.

a) Fartlek or speed play.
b) Sprinting 150 yards to 220 yards (4 to 6 times), resting 2 minutes.
c) Low and high hurdling (4 hurdles) 5 to 10 minutes.
d) Hopping from 50 to 100 yards. We do this on both legs 4 to 8 times.
e) Fast walking or jogging for 440 yards.
f) Striding for 100 yards (3 to 6 times).
g) Standing triple jump, working on all three parts of the event.
h) Early week workout—take 6 to 8 jumps.
i) Short sprints—take 5 to 8 (60-yard sprints).
j) Fast 300 yards—doing first 220 yards at a time 1 second slower than your best time—and all-out the last 80 yards.
k) Sprint starts with sprinters (8 to 10).

l) At end of week, run through marks (but no all-out effort of jumping).

NOTE: If you follow a good sprinters' or hurdlers' workout each night, plus your jumping, you won't be too far off a good workout for the triple jump. Don't forget the rope jumping, weights, circuit training and hopping.

TRIPS FOR THE TRIPLE JUMP

Following are some tips for the triple jump as illustrated in Figure 1:

The Approach: The approach should be no shorter than 135 feet, so you can get maximum controlled speed before you make the hop. You get your marks as you would in the long jump. The most important thing in the approach is which foot you plan on taking off on for the hop. Some feel you should use your strongest foot for the hop—this way you will be using it for two parts of the event. Others feel you should use your strongest leg to jump off of. We use the leg we feel the boy is going to improve the most with. We keep in mind that the hop will make or break your performance.

The Hop: As you approach for the hop, your body should be under controlled speed. For illustrative purposes, we will start the hop on the left foot.

a) The body should be erect; the head carried level and looking straight ahead (Figure 1a).

b) The left leg, which is being hopped on, should be fully extended for taking off after the hop. Balance is important here and the arms will help (Figure 1b).

c) Try for height on your hop—but if you cannot control it or lose your speed, it is better to lower height on hop.

d) After the hop, a hitch kick can be employed. As the right leg goes to the rear in the hitch kick, it should be straightened. The left leg is swung forward, knee high and foot ahead of knee (Figures 1c and 1d). The legs will be spread at this point (Figure 1d).

e) Now the left foot contacts the ground a little in front of the body weight. The body is erect and the arms are both coming through to help gain distance on the step (Figure 1e).

HOP   LANDING OF HOP

STEP   JUMP   LANDING

Figure 1—(a through l)

The Step: For the step, follow these tips:

a) From the contact of the left foot to the ground on the hop, the right knee has been swung through and brought up high to the chest. The body lean is forward (Figure 1f).

b) The right foot is then swung back and down and will hit the ground just in front of the body weight. The left leg should be trailing and both arms should be back ready to aid in the jump (Figure 1g).

c) Height is important in this part of the event and the arms should help here.

The Jump: For the jump, follow these tips:

a) From the contact of the foot on the steps, the rest of the event follows the long jump procedure (Figure 1h).

b) A hang or a hitch kick can be used in your final jump.

c) There should be good leg extension for landing; the arms should be swung back to aid in the landing. This way the jumper may be able to keep from sitting back in the pit (Figures 1j and 1k).

d) As the jumper hits the pit, the arms should be brought forward and the toes pointed down (Figure 1L).

NOTE: Many triple jumpers use ratios to guide their training. We start our jumpers this way but do not want it to be a must. A 10:7:10 ratio is used mostly. A 42' jump would take a 15'6" hop, an 11' step and a 15'6" jump. If you were shooting for 54', the ratio would have to be an 18'10" hop, a 16'4" step and a jump of 18'10". A good method for using the ratio is to mark everything out on your runway with sawdust. Then try to hit the marks with even and controlled speed.